RAINWATER HARVESTING:
A LIFELINE FOR HUMAN WELL-BEING

A report prepared for UNEP
by Stockholm Environment Institute

Fist published by United Nations Environment Programme and
Stockholm Environment Institute in 2009

Layout: Richard Clay/SEI

Cover photo: © ICRAF

Rainwater Harvesting - UNEP
ISBN: 978 - 92 - 807 - 3019 - 7
Job No. DEP/1162/NA

FOREWORD

In 2008 the world witnessed multiple crises including a food one which resulted in unrest in many areas of the world. These tensions may well foreshadow future challenges as they relate to providing sufficient food for six, rising to nine billion people. Unless we get more intelligent in the way we manage agriculture, the world is likely to head into deeply challenging times.

Water and the good and services provided by ecosystems are part of this urgent need for an intelligent management response not least in relation to food production.

The Millennium Ecosystems Assessment report, in which UNEP played an important role, demonstrated the links between healthy ecosystems and food production. These include providing food, water, fiber, genetic material; regulating soil erosion, purifying water and wastes, regulating floods, regulating diseases and pests; and supporting the formation of soil, photosynthesis and nutrient recycling.

Water is an integral part of ecosystems functioning. Its presence or absence has a bearing on the ecosystems services they provide. Relatively larger amounts of water are used to generate the ecosystem services needed to ensure provisioning of basic supplies of food, fodder and fibers. Today rainfed and irrigated agriculture use 7,600 of freshwater globally to provide food. An additional 1,600 km^3 of water is required annually to meet the millennium development goal on hunger reduction which addresses only half of the people suffering from hunger. This figure does not include water required for domestic, industrial and environmental (environmental flows. With renewable accessible freshwater globally limited to 12,500 km^3, the managing of water is a great challenge facing humanity. This makes it essential to find sustainable methods for managing water which incorporate all water users (environment, agriculture, domestic and industry) by promoting ecosystems management, resource efficiency, and governance and climate change adaptation.

There are numerous positive benefits for harvesting rainwater. The technology is low cost, highly decentralized empowering individuals and communities to manage their water. It has been used to improve access to water and sanitation at the local level. In agriculture rainwater harvesting has demonstrated the potential of doubling food production by 100% compared to the 10% increase from irrigation. Rainfed agriculture is practiced on 80% of the world's agricultural land area, and generates 65-70% of the world's staple foods. For instance in Africa more than 95% of the farmland is rainfed, almost 90% in Latin America.

The biggest challenge with using rainwater harvesting is that it is not included in water policies in many countries. In many cases water management is based on renewable water, which is surface and groundwater with little consideration of rainwater. Rainwater is taken as a 'free for all' resource and the last few years have seen an increase in its use. This has resulted in over abstracting, drastically reducing water downstream users including ecosystems. This has introduced water conflicts in some regions of the world. For the sustainable use of water resources, it is critical that rainwater harvesting is included as a water sources as is the case for ground wand surface water.

This publication highlights the link between rainwater harvesting, ecosystems and human well being and draws the attention of readers to both the negative and positive aspects of using this technology and how the negative benefits can be minimized and positive capitalized.

Achim Steiner

United Nations Under-Secretary General,
Executive Director,
United Nations Environment Programme

Editors:

Editor: Jennie Barron, Stockholm Environment Institute, York, UK/Stockholm Resilience Centre, Stockholm, Sweden
Reviewer: Mogens Dyhr-Nielsen, UNEP-DHI Collaborating Center, Hørsholm, Denmark
Changyeol Choi, UNEP-DEPI, Nairobi, Kenya

Chapter authors:

Jessica Calfoforo Salas, Kahublagan sang Panimalay Fnd, Iloilo City, Philippines
Luisa Cortesi, Megh Pyne Abhiyan, Bihar, India
Klaus W. König, Überlingen, Germany
Anders Malmer, Swedish University of Agricultural Sciences (SLU), Umeå, Sweden
Eklavya Prasad, Megh Pyne Abhiyan, Bihar, India
Bharat Sharma, International Water Management Institute, New Delhi, India

Contributing authors:

Mohamed Boufaroua. M, l'Aménagement et de la conservation des terres agricoles (ACTA), Tunis, Tunisie
Mohamed Bouitfirass, National Institute of Agronomic research (INRA), SETTAT, Morocco
Mogens Dyhr-Nielsen, UNEP-DHI Collaborating Center, Hørsholm, Denmark
Mohammed El Mourid, Centre International de Recherche Agricole dans les zones Sèches (ICARDA), Tunis, Tunisie
Johann Gnadlinger, Brazilian Rainwater Catchment and Management Association, (ABCMAC), Juazeiro, Brazil
Mooyoung Han, Seoul National University, Seoul, Republic of Korea
Günter Hauber-Davidson, Water Conservation Group Pty Ltd , Sydney, Australia
Harald Hiessl, Fraunhofer Institute for Systems and Innovation Research, Kalsruhe, Germany
Ulrik Ilstedt, Swedish University of Agricultural Sciences (SLU), Umeå, Sweden
Andrew Lo, Chinese Culture Univesity, Taipei, Taiwan
Farai Madziva, Harvest Ltd, Athi River, Kenya
Jean-Marc Mwenge Kahinda, Universityof Witwatersrand, Johannesburg, South Africa
Filbert B. Rwehumbiza, Sokoine University of Agriculture, Tanzania
Siza D. Tumbo, Sokoine University of Agriculture, Tanzania
Adouba ould Salem, Projet de développement pastoral et de gestion de parcours (PADEL), République Islamique de Mauritanie
Qiang Zhu, Gansu Research Institute for Water Conservacy, Wuxi City, China

CONTENTS

EXECUTIVE SUMMARY

1. Rainfall, ecosystems, and human well-being

Rainfall and soil water are fundamental parts of all terrestrial and aquatic ecosystems which supplies goods and services for human well-being. Availability and quality of water determines ecosystem productivity, both for agricultural and natural systems. There is increasing demand on water resources for development whilst maintaining healthy ecosystems, which put water resources under pressure. Ecosystem services suffer when rain and soil water becomes scarce due to changes from wet to dry seasons, or during within-seasonal droughts. Climate change, demand for development and already deteriorating state of ecosystems add to these pressures so that future challenges to sustain our ecosystems are escalating.

There is an immediate need to find innovative opportunities enabling development and human well-being without undermining ecosystem services. Among such opportunities one can ask: What potential can rainwater harvesting offer to enable increased human well-being whilst protecting our environment? What role can small-scale decentralised rainfall harvesting and storage play in integrated water resource management? And in which specific contexts may rainwater harvesting create synergies between good ecosystems management and human well-being? Rain water harvesting is the collective term for a wide variety of interventions to use rainfall through collection and storage, either in soil or in man-made dams, tanks or containers bridging dry spells and droughts. The effect is increased retention of water in the landscape, enabling management and use of water for multiple purposes.

2. Rainwater harvesting create synergies by upgrading rainfed agriculture and enhancing productive landscapes

Farms are undisputedly the most important ecosystems for human welfare. Rainfed agriculture provides nearly 60% of global food value on 72% of harvested land. Rainfall variability is an inherent challenge for farming in tropical and sub-tropical agricultural systems. These areas also coincide with many rural smallholder (semi-)subsistence farming systems, with high incidence of poverty and limited opportunities to cope with ecosystem changes. Water for domestic supply and livestock is irregular through temporal water flows and lowering ground water

in the landscape. The variable rainfall also result in poor crop water availability, reducing rainfed yields to 25-50% of potential yields, often less than 1 tonne cereal per hectare in South Asia and sub-Sahara Africa. The low agricultural productivity often offsets a negative spiral in landscape productivity, with degradation of ecosystem services through soil erosion, reduced vegetation cover, and species decline.

All vegetation uses rainwater, whether they are managed such as crops or tree plantations, or if they are natural forests, grasslands and shrubs. Often the ecosystems services from natural vegetation are not fully appreciated for its livelihood support until it is severely degraded, or disappeared, through for example, deforestation. Natural and permanent crop cover has the same effect as many rainwater harvesting interventions. By retaining landscape water flows, increased rainfall infiltration increase growth of vegetation, and decrease soil erosion, surface runoff and incidence flooding. Managing water resources in the landscape is thus management the permanent vegetation cover to enhance biomass production for fibres and energy, to harvest non-timber forest products and to enrich landscape biodiversity. Although forest and trees 'consumes' rainfall, they also safe-guard and generate many ecosystem services for livelihoods and economic good.

3. Mitigating floods and reducing pressures on water resources around urban areas

Today, more people live in urban areas than in rural areas globally. Cities can be considered as "artificial ecosystems", where controlled flows of water and energy provide a habitat for the urban population. Accordingly, the principles of ecosystem management also apply to sustainable urban water management. Rainwater harvesting has increasingly been promoted and implemented in urban areas for a variety of reasons. In Australia, withdrawals of water supply to the urban areas have been diminishing due to recurrent droughts. This has spurred private, commercial and public house-owners to invest in rainwater harvesting for household consumption. The increased use of rainwater harvesting provides additional water supply and reduce pressures of demand on surrounding surface and groundwater resources. In parts of Japan and South Korea, rainwater harvesting with storage has been implemented also as a way to reduce vulnerability in emergencies, such as earth quakes or severe flooding which can disrupt public water supply. The effect of multiple rainwater harvesting interventions on ecosystem services in urban areas are two-fold. Firstly, it can reduce pressures of demand on surrounding surface and groundwater resources. Secondly, the rainwater harvesting interventions can reduce storm flow, decreasing incidence of flooding and short peak flows.

4 Climate change adaptation and the role of rainwater harvesting

Climate change will affect rainfall and increase evaporation, which will put increasing pressures on our ecosystems services. At the same time, development by a growing population will affect our ecosystems as we increase our demands for services, including reliable and clean water. Rainwater harvesting will continue to be an adaptation strategy for people living with high rainfall variability, both for domestic supply and to enhance crop, livestock and other forms of agriculture.

5. Enabling the benefits of rainwater harvesting

The rainwater use by crops and natural vegetation is in many cases by-passed in integrated water resource management (IWRM), which primarily focus on streamflow or groundwater resources. Consequently, the rainwater harvesting interventions are not widely recognised in water policy or in investment plans, despite the broad base of cases identifying multiple benefits for development and sustainability. By introducing policies recognising the value of ecosystem services and the role of rainfall to support these systems, rain water harvesting emerges as a set of interventions addressing multiple issues on human well-being and improved ecosystems services. The extensive interventions of rainwater harvesting in for example India, China, Brazil, and Australia have occurred where governments and communities jointly make efforts in enabling policies and legislation, together with cost-sharing and subsidises for rainwater harvesting interventions.

Rainwater harvesting will affect the landscape water flows, and subsequently the landscape ecosystem services. If the collected water is used solely for consumptive use, as by crops and trees, the trade-off of alternative water use has to be considered. If the water is mostly used as domestic supply, most water will re-enter the landscape at some stage, possibly in need of purification

Rainwater harvesting has in many cases not only increased human well-being and ecosystem services, but also acted as a way of improving equity, gender balance and strengthen social capital in a community. To improve domestic water supply with rainwater harvesting interventions, save women and children from the tedious work of fetching water. It also improves household sanitation and health. The value of community organisation enabled through implementation of rainwater harvesting in the watershed has strengthen communities to address other issues relation to development, health and knowledge in their livelihoods and environment. These are important benefits which can further help individuals and communities to improve both ecosystems management as well as human well-being.

6. Suggestions:

- Consider rainfall as an important manageable resource in water management policies, strategies and plans. Then rainwater harvesting interventions are included as a potential option in land and water resource management for human well-being and ecosystems productivity.

- Realize that rainwater harvesting is not a 'silver bullet', but it can be efficient as a complementary and viable alternative to large-scale water withdrawals, and reduce negative impacts on ecosystems services, not least in emerging water-stressed basin

- Rainwater harvesting is a local intervention with primarily local benefits on ecosystems and human livelihoods. Stakeholder consultation and public participation are key to negotiate positive and negative trade-offs potentially emerging, comparing rainwater harvesting interventions with alternative water management interventions.

- Access and right to land can be a first step to rainwater harvesting interventions. Special measures should be in place so rainwater harvesting interventions also benefit land-poor and landless in a community

- Establish enabling policies and cost –sharing strategies, (including subsides) to be provided together with technical know-how and capacity building.

CHAPTER 1

INTRODUCTION: RAINWATER HARVESTING AS A WAY TO SUPPORT ECOSYSTEM SERVICES AND HUMAN WELL-BEING

Author: Jennie Barron, Stockholm Environment Institute, York, UK/Stockholm Resilience Centre, Stockholm, Sweden

Ecosystem services are fundamental for human well-being. Our health, livelihoods and economies rely on well functioning ecosystem services which range from provision of ambience and recreational opportunities to flood storage and pollution assimilation. Availability of water is critical for ecosystem health and productivity, ensuring supply of a range of products and services, to benefit human well-being (e.g., GEO4, 2007; MA, 2005) With growing multiple demands of water, the ecosystems supporting and regulating the structure and function of natural ecosystems may be eroding (WRI et al., 2005; WRI *et al.*, 2008). There is an urgent need to find opportunities to enable development and promote human well-being without undermining ecosystem health. What opportunities can rainwater harvesting offer to enable sustainable development, increase human well-being, and environmental protection?

Rainwater harvesting locally collects and stores rainfall through different technologies, for future use to meet the demands of human consumption or human activities. The art of rainwater harvesting has been practised since the first human settlements. It has been a key entry point in local water management ever since, buffering supplies of rainfall to service the human demand of freshwater. As it involves the alteration of natural landscape water flows, it requires water managers to carefully consider the tradeoffs; however, it can create multiple benefits, offering synergies between different demands and users at a specific location (Malesu *et al.*, 2005: Agarwal *et al.*, 2005). To many water managers, rainwater harvesting is a technique to collect drinking water from rooftops, or to collect irrigation water in rural water tanks. However, rainwater harvesting has much wider perspectives, in particular if it is considered in relation to its role in supporting ecosystem goods and services.

Future pressures from climate change, growing population, rapid landuse changes and already degraded water resources quality, may intensify water shortages in specific communities and exacerbate existing environmental and economic concerns. As growing pressure mounts on our water resources, globally and locally, we need to manage resources more efficiently in order to meet multiple demands and purposes. What are examples of 'good practices' in water management? Are the effective pathways for development known, that meet multiple demands whilst avoiding negative ecosystems impacts?

In this report, the concept of rainwater harvesting is examined for its potential to increase human well-being without eroding the ecosystems functions that water serves in the local landscape. Examples from diverse geographical and societal settings are examined, to demonstrate the benefits and constraints of rainwater harvesting technologies in addressing multiple demands for freshwater in specific locations The aim is to compile a synthesis of experiences that can provide insight into the multiple opportunities rainwater harvesting can have when addressing human well-being, while continuing to sustain a range of ecosystem services.

1.1 SCOPE

This synthesis of linkages between ecosystem services, human well-being and rainwater harvesting interventions examines 29 cases from diverse economic and environmental settings. The cases were selected to present economic activities (like forestry, agriculture, watershed development and, rural and urban development) in relation to different rainwater harvesting technologies, water uses, and hydro-climatic and economic settings (Fig. 1.1). The indicators of impacts on ecosystems are described using the overarching framework of the Millennium Ecosystem

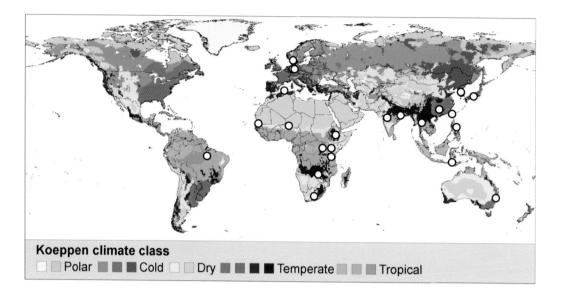

Figure 1.1: Case studies of rainwater harvesting implementation presented in the publication

Assessment (MA, 2005), applied to identify key water-related issues (GEO4, 2007). The human well-being indicators used directly stem from the Millennium Development Goals and targets (UN MDG web sites, 2009; UN Millennium Declaration, 2000).

1.2 ORGANISATION OF THIS REPORT

This report systematically synthesises the close links between human well-being and ecosystem services through a number of rainwater harvesting cases. The cases are organised into thematic chapters addressing rainwater harvesting systems, their roles and their impacts (Fig. 1.2; Chapter 3-7; Appendix II). The chapter themes were selected based on the economic importance of the specific themes for human well-being and contain examples in which rainwater harvesting has, and may continue to play, an integral role. The cases were selected to represent a wide variety of social, economic and hydro-climatic conditions. They exemplify a diverse set of rainwater harvesting technologies, and uses of the collected water.

The report synthesises the positive and negative impacts of the rainwater harvesting cases (Chapter 8), using a pre-defined set of indicators of ecosystems impacts and human well-being. The outcomes are interpreted in a number of key messages and recommendations (Chapter 9).

REFERENCES

A. Agarwal A.,and S. Narain . 2005. Dying wisdom: Rise, fall and potential of India's traditional water harvesting systems 4th edition. . Eds., State of Indias Environment, a citizens' report 4, Centre for Science and Environment, New Delhi, (404 pp)

GEO4. 2007. Global Environmental Outlook 4: Environment for development. United Nations Environment Programme, Nairobi/ Progress Press, Malta

Malesu, M, Oduor, A.R., Odhiambo, O.J. eds. 2008. Green water management handbook: rainwater harvesting for agricultural production and ecological sustainability Nairobi, Kenya : World Agroforestry Centre ICRAF 229p.

Millennium Ecosystems Assessment (MA). 2005. Ecosystems and human well-being: synthesis. Island Press, Washington D.C.

United Nations Millennium Development Goal Indicators (UN MDG). 2009. Official web site for monitoring MDG indicators. http://unstats.un.org/unsd/mdg/Default.aspx *Last accessed January 2009*

UN Millennium Declaration, 2000. Resolution adopted by the General Assembly (A/RES/55/2) 18/09/2000

World Resources Institute (WRI) with United Nations Development Programme, United Nations Environment Programme, World Bank. 2005. The

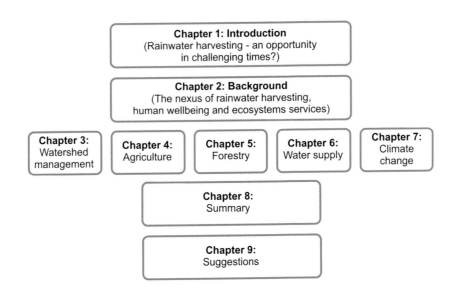

Figure 1.2: Readers guide to this report on rainwater harvesting, ecosystems and human well-being.

Wealth of the Poor: Managing Ecosystems to Fight Poverty. Washington D.C. , WRI

World Resources Institute (WRI) with United Nations Development Programme, United Nations Environment Programme, World Bank. 2008. World Resources 2008: Roots of Resilience - Growing the Wealth of the Poor. Washington D.C.

CHAPTER 2

BACKGROUND: THE WATER COMPONENT OF ECOSYSTEM SERVICES AND IN HUMAN WELL-BEING DEVELOPMENT TARGETS

Author: Jennie Barron, Stockholm Environment Institute, York, UK/Stockholm Resilience Centre, Stockholm, Sweden

2.1 RAINWATER HARVESTING AND ECOSYSTEM SERVICES:

Rain water harvesting, water flows and ecosystem services

Rainwater harvesting is often an intervention intended to augment the Provisioning Services of the environment for human well-being. Provisioning Services, as defined in the Millennium Ecosystem Assessment, include environmental services such as improved and safe water supplies, or increased crop production. A closer analysis shows that rainwater harvesting often has many more impacts, both positive and negative on ecosystem services, and extending to regulating, cultural and supporting services (Table 2.1).

Provisioning ecosystem services and rainwater harvesting: Water is essential for all living beings, for consumptive use. Plants and vegetation are by far the largest water consumers, but they also provide direct livelihood and economic returns to humans as food, fodder, fibres and timber, in addition to products for pharmaceutical use, diverse genetic resources and fresh water.. Abstraction of water for human use is circa 3,600 km3, or 25 % of renewable freshwater flows annually (MA, 2005). These abstractions mainly provide irrigation water (70%) to increase crop production. Use of water for drinking, and public, commercial and other societal needs is essential but relatively minor in quantity, and much is returned to landscape, often through waste water systems.

▶ Rainwater harvesting is a way of increasing the provisioning capacity at a specific location. Many rainwater harvesting interventions to date are primarily to increase crop/fodder/food/timber production, or to provide domestic/public/commercial supplies of water.

Regulating ecosystem services and rainwater harvesting: The regulating services are in addition

Table 2.1: Ecosystems functions and the effect of rainwater harvesting

Ecosystem services	Effect of rainwater harvesting intervention...
Provisioning	can increase crop productivity, food supply and income can increase water and fodder for livestock and poultry can increase rainfall infiltration, thus recharging shallow groundwater sources and base flow in rivers can regenerate landscapes increasing biomass, food, fodder, fibre and wood for human consumption improves productive habitats, and increases species diversity in flora and fauna
Regulating	can affect the temporal distribution of water in landscape reduces fast flows and reduces incidences of flooding reduces soil erosion can provide habitat for harmful vector diseases bridges water supply in droughts and dry spells
Cultural	rain water harvesting and storage of water can support spiritual, religious and aesthetic values creates green oasis/mosaic landscape which has aesthetic value
Supporting	can enhance the primary productivity in landscape can help support nutrient flows in landscape, including water purification

to the supporting services, discussed below, and are essential for human well-being as they control the type and provisioning capacity of ecosystems in specific locations. Water flows across the landscape play a role in a range of regulation services as water is primarily involved in many of them. The primary roles of the presence (or absence) of water are in erosion control, climatic control, pest and disease control (through habitat regulation), water quality control and control of natural hazards.

▶ Implementation of rainwater harvesting interventions may affect the regulating services of the landscape as the landscape water flows change. As mentioned earlier, soil conservation measures to reduce soil erosion also act as *in situ* rainwater harvesting measures. *Ex situ* rainwater harvesting and storage in the urban and rural landscape affects flooding and flow duration over seasons. Increasing the numbers of ponds and dams storing harvested rainwater in the landscape may increase the incidence of malaria, but if covered, or if water is stored underground, this may not impact incidence of malaria in the specific location.

Cultural ecosystem services and rainwater harvesting: Water has strong cultural and religious values. These values are critical for human spiritual well-being, and are recognised as having an essential role in societal interactions, once primary resources are provided. Water also has an aesthetic value, enhancing garden and ornamental plant growth, and providing green "oases," for example, in urban areas.

▶ Increasing access to water through rainwater harvesting in a community or household may act to enhance the access and ability to carry out religious and spiritual rituals. It can also increase the aesthetic use of water. At the landscape scale, water features are often protected and given specific values and protection by the local community.

Supporting ecosystem services: The supporting services pre-determine the conditions for all other services. Water flows play an essential role as a medium for the transport of nutrients and contaminants, in the shaping of soils, and in photosynthesis. Together with soil conditions and climate conditions the water balance will determine the net primary production level at a given location.

▶ Rainwater harvesting will not primarily affect these supporting services. Indirectly, soil formation may change from a natural course as *in situ* management interventions are implemented. Also leakage of nutrients may change, but indirectly, mainly due to changing from natural landuse patterns to agricultural uses rather than from implementing *in situ* rainwater harvesting in the fields.

To conclude, rainwater harvesting is often implemented to improve local provisioning capacity by ecosystems for human well-being. However, as the landscape water balance is affected by increased rainwater harvesting, other services, in particular regulating services related to water abundance and availability, can be affected. Cultural services can be either negatively (if resources are diminished due to rainwater harvesting) or positively, depending on the local context.

Water flows in the landscape and effects of rainwater harvesting

Rainfall is the main source of freshwater in all land-based ecosystems, whether natural or managed by humans. From arid deserts to the humid tropical rainforests, the flow of water through the ecosystem shapes the characteristic fauna and flora as well as the soil systems. The land surfaces globally receive 113,000 km^3 of rainfall. Of this, approximately 41,000 km^3 (36%) is manifested as surface runoff in the liquid phase—the so-called 'blue water' of rivers, streams and lakes. The remaining amount, 64%, of the rainfall, is evaporated through vegetation, from soil surfaces and from water surfaces within the landscape.

Rainwater harvesting is principally the management of these two partitioning points in the water flow. At the local scale, such as a farm field, the flows partition the incoming rainfall at the soil surface, either infiltrating the water into the soil or diverting the water as surface runoff (Fig. 2.1). Within the soil, the second partitioning point is at the plant roots where water is either taken up by the vegetation, or contributes to the recharge of shallow or deep groundwater. Depending on the soil surface conditions, infiltration can range from 100% in a well managed agricultural soil, to 100% runoff from a paved road or rooftop. The second partitioning point can be managed, indirectly, through planting different plant species, improving crop uptake capacity, modifying plant root depths, and altering soil management practices in agriculture, through enhancing/depleting soil health, including soil organic matter content. *In situ* rainwater harvesting interventions (Fig. 2.1) address both partitioning points at the field scale. Many soil management practises, such as soil conservation measures that enhance the soil infiltration capacity and soil moisture storage, can alter the partitioning process. Practises that enhance root water uptake for crop growth act as an '*in situ* rainwater harvesting' intervention. *Ex situ* rainwater harvesting, in contrast, alters the partitioning process at the local field scale.

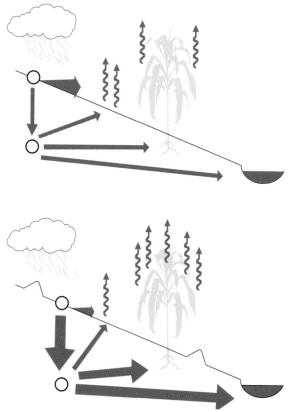

Figure 2.1: Landscape water balance flows a) without rainwater harvesting, and b) an example of flow paths with rain water harvesting interventions with water partitioning points at the soil surface (1), and in the soil (2). Rainwater harvesting is principally about managing water partitioning in these points.

At the landscape scale (or meso-scale, 1 km²-10,000 km²), rainfall partitioning and flow paths are the same as at the field scale, but the quantities cannot simply be aggregated from field scale to landscape scale, as water often re-distributes itself within the field, and/or along a slope gradient. When rainwater harvesting interventions

are implemented, the partitioning is changed. One change is to increase infiltration and storage of water in the soil. This has short term advantages (based on a single rainfall event) as it slows the flow of water, which reduces soil erosion, minimizes flooding and limits damage to built structures due to storm water flows (Fig. 2.2). A longer term advantage (on the scale of days to months) is an effect of the slower flows of water within the landscape. The longer residence times enable water to be accessed during dry periods, and used for productive purposes, including human consumption, livestock watering and increased crop and vegetation growth.

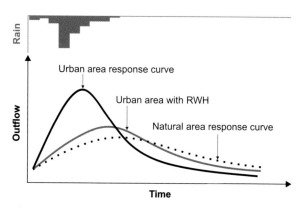

Figure 2.2: principal flow response curve from an urban catchment with and without rainwater harvesting in place, showing the effect of slower flow through the landscape (contributed by K. König)

While rainwater harvesting can increase crop and other vegetation productivity through improved water access, reducing soil erosion and incidences of flooding downstream, harvested rainfall may increase depletion of downstream users' access to water conveyed downstream as surface runoff or downgradient as groundwater. At a certain point, if the consumptive use of water resources such as for crop or other vegetation growth is complete, the loss of downstream access to the water may be severe and irreversible (Box 2.1). Further interventions may affect the landscape water flows so it is impossible to restore downstream or downgradient access, i.e., the water balance undergoes a regime shift. Such regime shifts include altering the timing of delivery of surface runoff, for example when deforestation or afforestation occurs, or when irrigated agriculture affects groundwater levels and/or water quality (through salinization, for example). Shifts in flow regimes are difficult to remediate. To date, there is

Box 2.1: Managing regime shifts in landscape water balances

Increasingly, it is recognised that the multiple interventions by humans on ecosystems sometimes create unexpected and irretrievable changes in the services provided. These unexpected changes are often referred to as 'tipping points', where an ecosystem or its services shift from one production regime to another. In water resource management such tipping points have been experienced in watershed and river basins subject to excessive consumptive and re-allocation of water resources (example left hand figure). An example is the Aral Sea, which due to irrigation water outtake, is permanently damaged with concomitant reductions in ecosystem services generated. At a smaller scale, excessive erosion can

alter a field to an unproductive state, and, with a single event, possibly irretrievably damage the field through land subsidence or a landslide. With increasing interventions to abstract water, communities and resource managers should be aware that interventions at different scales can feedback unexpectedly, and erode ecosystem services permanently. On the other hand, efficient and productive water and land usage, for example through many small-scale rainwater harvesting interventions, has shown positive change, where interventions have resulted in increased opportunity and productivity of ecosystem services (right hand figure, case a).

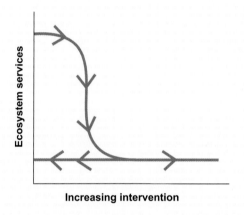

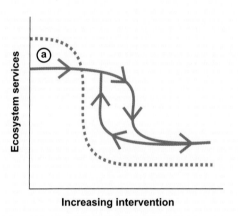

limited synthesised evidence to document the impact of rainwater harvesting on downstream water flows (Box 2.2).

2.2 RAINWATER AND HUMAN WELL-BEING

Water as an essential good for human well-being

Water is an essential commodity for all living beings: for direct consumption to sustain life and health, for indirect consumption through water required to grow food, fodder and fibres, and for maintenance of the range of ecosystem services needed to support and sustain economic and social activities. Water's role in promoting human well-being has been variously

defined.[1] Four key areas stand out as particularly important when linking water with improvements of human well-being:

1 For example, the 2006 Human Development Report (UNDP, 2006), which focuses on water, divides water's role in human well-being into two categories: water for life (drinking water, sanitation, health) and water for livelihoods (water scarcity, risk and vulnerability; water for agriculture); a Poverty Environment Partnership paper (ADB *et al.*, 2006) looks at four dimensions through which water can impact poverty and human well-being: through livelihoods, health, vulnerability to natural hazards and pro-poor economic growth; and the World Water Assessment Programme (UNESCO, 2006) considers:

Box 2.2: Potential impacts on stream flow of rainwater harvesting in South Africa

In the last two decades, rainwater harvesting has been have been implemented in the rural areas of South Africa to help address the Millennium Development Goals. As South Africa is increasingly water stressed, it is important to ensure flows for healthy rivers and streams as well as water supply for humans. By using a decision support tool (RHADESS) for evaluating rainwater harvestingoptions, both indications of suitability and potential impacts can be assessed. Application to two watersheds showed that the suitability of *in situ* or *ex situ* rainwater harvesting ranged from 14% to 67% of the area served. The impact of different levels of rainwater harvesting (0,

50, 100 %) was compared to long-term naturalised flows. The results showed that both *in situ* and *ex situ* rainwater harvesting caused marginal to major decreases in runoff compared with the runoff from the virgin catchment (natural vegetation), depending on adoption rate. It also showed that different technologies impact different flow regimes. The *in situ* rain water harvesting technique has a relatively greater impact on high flows, while *ex situ* interventions have a greater impact on low flows.

J. Mwenge Kahinda *et al.*, 2008 (Case 2.1)

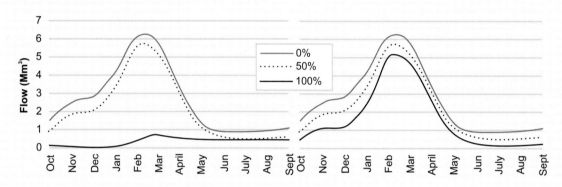

- water and health: domestic water supplies for human consumption, hygiene and sanitation;

- water and basic provisioning: water for producing food, fodder and fibres;

- water and livelihoods: water to support rural livelihoods and sustain economic activity; and

- water and vulnerability: water as a component in natural disasters and disaster mitigation.

water for health; water in food, agriculture and for rural livelihoods; water in the energy and industrial sectors; and water and risk management. Further, there are other definitions of the dimensions of human well-being, for example in the MA (2005), which points out five key areas: basic material for a good life, freedom and choice, health, good social relations and security. Further, the MEA addresses the issue of well-functioning ecosystems being a pre-requisite to enable the development of these basic human well-being aspects.

A globally accepted set of indicators of human well-being are the Millennium Development Goals and associated targets, which were developed and agreed in 2000 (UN Millennium Declaration, 2000). Rainwater harvesting can play both a direct and indirect role in the achievement of many of these goals (Table 2.2), particularly in the area of basic human needs and health. A more comprehensive view of human well-being is taken by the Millennium Ecosystem Assessment (MA, 2005) in which human well-being is not only a result of good health and adequate basic provision of food, shelter and other material necessities, but also related to freedom of choice and action, security and the need for good social relations (MA, 2005). In this context several cases of rainwater harvesting, especially as an element in watershed management, can play a significant role, especially for social relations, where water management has long been a unifying factor. There is increasing evidence that watershed management with rain water harvesting has strengthened social capital which in turn can have a significant impact on development of other ecosystem services for human well-being (e.g., Joshi *et al.*, 2005; Kerr, 2002; Barron *et al.*, 2007).

The Millennium Development Goals: increasing pressure on water and ecosystem services?

Several MDGs are closely related to water for health and sanitation. The MDG Target 7C aims to halve water supply deficits, presenting a formidable challenge for investment and social and technical alignment. However, the amounts of water necessary to reduce water supply deficits are in many cases available. In addition, the use of domestic water is not necessarily consumptive, as the water can be cleaned and re-used. Quantifying minimum water requirements to meet basic human needs has resulted in vastly disparate estimates. Annual per capita water needs range between 18 m^3 and 49 m^3, suggesting that approximately 0.1 to 0.3 km^3 is required for basic water consumption, sanitation and societal uses by the global population. It is important to note that water for domestic, public and commercial use in many cases is returned to stream flow locally. Return flows are reduced by consumptive losses, and often result in diminished water quality, increased health risks amongst downstream users and degraded habitats.

Relatively larger amounts of water are used to generate the ecosystem services needed to ensure provisioning of basic supplies of food, fodder and fibres. Just to meet the food requirements of a balanced diet, approximately 1,300-1,800 m^3 of water per person are consumed per year. This translates to 8,800-12,200 km^3 for a world population of 6.7 billion in 2008/2009. The water used for food production, whether irrigated or rainfed, is consumptive; i.e., at a local site, water will be incorporated into foodstuffs, evaporated from the land surface or otherwise non-retrievable for further use downstream. In comparison with amounts of water needed for domestic, public and commercial purposes, the projected needs for additional water to meet MDG target on hunger (MDG 1C) suggest additional withdrawals of water for both rainfed and irrigated agriculture to meet the target through 2015. Today, rainfed and irrigated agriculture appropriate 7,700 km^3 of freshwater globally to provide food (CA, 2007). Of this, approximately 2,600 km^3 is direct withdrawals for irrigation purposes. To meet the MDG Hunger goal, an additional volume of 1,850 to 2,200 km^3 of water needs to be appropriated annually, based upon current agricultural practises and assuming balanced diets (Fig. 2.3; SEI, 2005). To feed all a reasonable diet by 2050 may require almost doubling of today's water resources. With renewable accessible freshwater globally limited to 12,500 km^3, it is a great challenge facing humanity. The consumptive use of water for crops and vegetation to provide other biomass goods such as timber, fibres for clothing, wood for energy etc. is not included in the above numbers.

A third dimension is the sustainable management of resources. This is mainly addressed in MDG 7 (Target 7a: Integrate sustainable natural resource strategies in national policies). This target can be interpreted as seeking to ensure sustainable use and safeguarding of water resources. Such safeguarding could include the management of water for other uses, for example, for ecosystem services, including provision of minimal environmental flows necessary for maintenance of aquatic organisms and their habitats. Accounting for the provision of minimum environmental flows in major river basins suggests that water stress is even more imminent than when estimated based on renewable water resources solely for human use (Smakthin *et al.*, 2004; Fig. 2.4). These estimates suggest that, already, 1.1 billion people are living in severely water stressed basins (0.9<Water Stress Index<1), and an additional 700 million people live in moderately stressed river basins (0.6<Water Stress Index<0.9). Clearly, further consumptive use of water or increased pollution may seriously affect ecosystem health, as well as human well-being and potential for development.

2.3 RAINWATER HARVESTING: WHAT IS IT?

Definition and typology of rainwater harvesting systems

Rainwater harvesting consists of a wide range of technologies used to collect, store and provide water with the particular aim of meeting demand for water by humans and/or human activities (Fig. 2.5 cf. Malesu *et al.*, 2005; Ngigi, 2003; SIWI, 2001).

These technologies can be divided into two main areas depending on source of water collected; namely, the *in situ* and the *ex situ* types of rainwater harvesting, respectively. In essence, *in situ* rainwater harvesting

Table 2.2: The Millennium Development Goals (UN MDG, 2009) and the role of rainwater harvesting

Millennium Development Goal	Role of rainwater harvesting	Relevance
1. End poverty and hunger	can act as an entry point to improve agricultural production, regenerate degraded landscapes and supply water for small horticulture and livestock can improve incomes and food security	Primary
2. Universal education	can reduce time devoted to tedious water fetching activities, enabling more time for schooling	Secondary
3. Gender equality	interventions have been shown to improve gender equality and income group equity by reducing the time spent by women gathering water for domestic purposes provides water so that girls can attend school even during theirr menstrual cycles, thus increasing school attendance	Primary
4. Child health	contributes to better domestic water supply and improves sanitation reducing the incidence of water borne diseases which are the major cause of deaths among the under fives	Primary
5. Maternal health	can supply better quality domestic water, which helps suppress diarrhoea etc. can release time from tedious water fetching activities	Secondary
6. Combat HIV/AIDS	no direct linkages	Secondary
7. Environmental sustainability	interventions provide fresh water for humans and livestock can regenerate ecosystem productivity and suppress degradation of services by soil erosion and flooding rainwater harvesting can improve environmental flows by increasing base flow where groundwater is recharged	Primary
8. Global partnership	rainwater management is part of IWRM which is transnational issue	Secondary

technologies are soil management strategies that enhance rainfall infiltration and reduce surface runoff. The *in situ* systems have a relatively small rainwater harvesting catchment typically no greater than 5-10 m from point of water infiltration into the soil. The rainwater capture area is within the field where the crop is grown (or point of water infiltration). *In situ* systems are also characterised by the soil being the storage medium for the water. This has two principal effects. Firstly, it is difficult to control outtake of the water over time. Normally soil moisture storage for crop uptake is 5-60 days, depending on vegetation type, root depth and temperatures in soil and overlying atmosphere. Secondly, the outtake in space is determined by the soil medium characteristics, including slope. Due to gradients and sub-surface conditions, the harvested water can act as recharge for more distant water sources in the landscape, including groundwater, natural water ways and wetlands, and shallow wells. The *in situ* rainwater harvesting systems are often identical to a range of soil conservation measures, such as terracing, pitting, conservation tillage practices, commonly implemented to counter soil erosion. Thus, harvesting

rainwater by increasing soil infiltration using *in situ* technologies also counteracts soil loss from the farmed fields or forested areas. *In situ* rainwater harvesting often serves primarily to recharge soil water for crop and other vegetation growth in the landscape. The water can also be used for other purposes, including livestock and domestic supplies if it serves to recharge shallow groundwater aquifers and/or supply other water flows in the landscape.

The *ex situ* systems are defined as systems which have rainwater harvesting capture areas external to the point of water storage. The rainwater capture area varies from being a natural soil surface with a limited infiltration capacity, to an artificial surface with low or no infiltration capacity. Commonly used impermeable surfaces are rooftops, roads and pavements, which can generate substantial amounts of water and which can be fairly easily collected and stored for different uses. As the storage systems of *ex situ* systems often are wells, dams, ponds or cisterns, water can be abstracted easily for multiple uses including for crops and other vegetation as irrigation water, or for domestic, public and

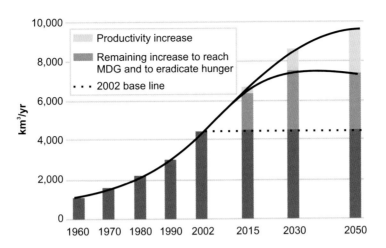

Figure 2.3: The additional required water input needed to meet the Millennium Development Goal on halving hunger 2015, and projections of water needed for eradicating hunger globally in 2050 (SEI, 2005).

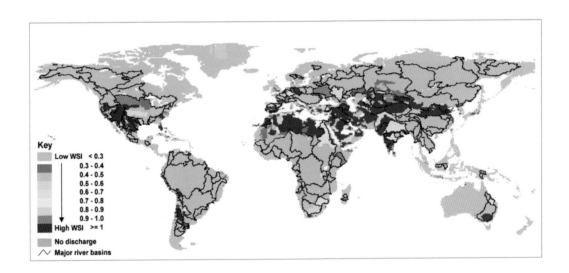

Figure 2.4: Water stressed areas of the world accounting for environmental flows in river basins. Values of the Water Stress Index 0.6<WSI<1 indicates potentially major impact on ecosystem services if further withdrawals are made

Smakthin et al., 2004

commercial uses through centralised or decentralised distribution systems. By collecting and storing water in dams, tanks, and cisterns the storage time is more dependent on the size of capture area, size of storage unit and rate of outtake rather than residence time and flow gradient through the soil.

The wide variety of rainwater harvesting technologies and end uses of the water also indicates the dynamic and flexible dimensions of rainwater harvesting systems. They also reflect the multiple end uses of the water collected for our benefit, including agriculture and landscape management, domestic, public and commercial water supply, as well as livestock watering, aquaculture and maintaining aesthetic values.

Current and potential implementation of rainwater harvesting systems

There is much historical evidence of rainwater harvesting being an important factor in community development since the beginning of human settlements. Many cultures have developed their societies with the primary management of water resources as a corner stone, developing more sophisticated ways of supplying water both for consumption and agriculture. Rainwater harvesting structures using cisterns are dated as early as 3000 BC in the Middle East. A more in-depth description of ancient rainwater harvesting in India has been summarised by the Centre for Science and Environment, India (Agarwal and Narain, 2005).

At the global level, there is no comprehensive assessment of the extent of implementation of rainwater harvesting technologies for specific uses. Nor is there any summarized information on how much land is currently under any type of *in situ* rainwater harvesting. For the specific application of conservation tillage, as no tillage agriculture, national statistics have been aggregated by Hobbs *et al.* (2008). Their information suggests that, globally, only a small fraction of the land surface, amounting to about 95 million hectares, is currently under conservation or no–till agriculture.

For irrigation and conservation tillage, the AQUASTAT data base (FAO, 2009) holds data for a selected number of countries. Unfortunately, the information on irrigation cannot directly be associated with rainwater harvesting systems for irrigation purposes as it differentiates between surface water and groundwater, which does not allow the separation of shallow groundwater from deep groundwater, nor surface water withdrawn from 'blue' water sources (lakes, water ways, large dams) from smaller scale systems. The recent assessment

of irrigated and rainfed land, completed in the Comprehensive Assessment of Water Management in Agriculture (CA, 2007), also did not differentiate areas under rainwater harvested water supply from areas under other types of water supply for irrigation. This lack of global information on where and how much rainwater harvesting is currently in use makes it impossible to say how many people actually benefit from rainwater harvesting today. It also becomes challenging to summarize the global and/or regional benefits and costs in specific locations, countries or regions of rainwater harvesting for human well-being or ecosystem impacts arising from rainwater harvesting.

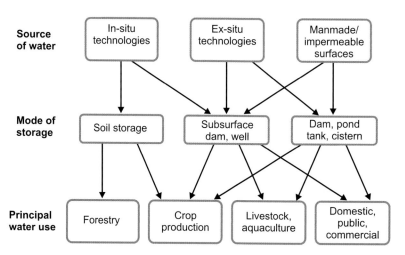

Figure 2.5: Schematic of rainwater harvesting technologies based on source of water and water storage type

Modified after SIWI, 2001

REFERENCES

AQUASTAT. 2009. AQUATSTAT online. FAO, Rome, http://www.fao.org/nr/water/aquastat/dbase/index.stm

Barron, J., Noel, S. *et al.* 2008. Agricultural water management in smallholder farming systems: the value of soft components in meso-scale interventions. SEI Project Report, Stockholm Environment Institute, Stockholm (38 p)

Agarwal A.,and S. Narain . 2005. Dying wisdom: Rise, fall and potential of India's traditional water harvesting systems 4th edition. . Eds., State of Indias Environment, a citizens' report 4, Centre for Science and Environment, New Delhi, (404 pp)

GEO4. 2007. Global Environmental Outlook 4: Environment for development. United Nations Environment Programme, Nairobi/ Progress Press, Malta

Hobbs, P., Sayre, K., Gupta,R. 2008. The role of conservation agriculture in sustainable agriculture. Phil Trans R. Soc. B 363:543-555

Joshi, P.K., Jha, A. K., Wani, S.P., Joshi, Laxmi and Shiyani, R. L. 2005. Meta-analysis to assess impact of watershed program and people's participation. Comprehensive Assessment Research Report 8. Comprehensive Assessment Secretariat Colombo, Sri Lanka.

Kerr, J.M., 2002b. Watershed development projects in India: an evaluation. Research Report 127,. IFPRI, Washington, DC.

Malesu, M, Oduor, A.R., Odhiambo, O.J. eds. 2008. Green water management handbook: rainwater harvesting for agricultural production and ecological sustainability Nairobi, Kenya : World Agroforestry Centre ICRAF 229p.

Millennium Ecosystems Assessment (MA). 2005. Ecosystems and human well-being: synthesis. Island Press, Washington D.C.

Millennium Ecosystems Assessment (MA). Ecosystems and human well-being: Current states and trends Chapter 5. Ecosystem conditions and human well-being.(Eds. Hassan, Scholes and Ash), Island Press, Washington D.C.

Poverty-Environment Partnership (PEP). 2006. Linking poverty reduction and water management. UNEP –SEI publication for the Poverty-Environment Partnership, http://www.povertyenvironment.net/pep/

SEI, 2005. Sustainable pathways to attain the millennium development goals - assessing the role of water, energy and sanitation. Document prepared for the UN World Summit, Sept 14, 2005, New York. Stockholm Environment Institute, Stockholm http://www.sei.se/mdg.htm

SIWI. 2001. Water harvesting for upgrading rainfed agriculture: Problem analysis and research needs. SIWI Report 11, Stockholm (101p)

Smakthin, V.U., Revenga, C., Döll, P. 2004. Taking into account environmental water requirements in global-scale water resources assessments. Research Report of the CGIAR Comprehensive Assessment of Water Management in Agriculture. No. 2, International Water Management Institute, Colombo, Sri Lanka, 24 pp

United Nations Millennium Development Goal Indicators (UN MDG). 2009. Official web site for monitoring MDG indicators. http://unstats.un.org/unsd/mdg/Default.aspx *Last accessed January 2009*

UN Millennium Declaration, 2000. Resolution adopted by the General Assembly (A/RES/55/2) 18/09/2000

World Resources Institute (WRI) with United Nations Development Programme, United Nations Environment Programme, World Bank. 2005. The Wealth of the Poor: Managing Ecosystems to Fight Poverty. Washington D.C. , WRI

World Resources Institute (WRI) with United Nations Development Programme, United Nations Environment Programme, World Bank. 2008. World Resources 2008: Roots of Resilience - Growing the Wealth of the Poor. Washington D.C. WRI

CHAPTER 3

RAINWATER HARVESTING FOR MANAGEMENT OF WATERSHED ECOSYSTEMS

Main author: Luisa Cortesi, Eklavya Prasad, Megh Pyne Abhiyan, Bihar, India

Contributing authors: Mogens Dyhr-Nielsen, UNEP-DHI Collaborating Center, Hørsholm, Denmark

3.1 THE ROLE OF WATERSHED MANAGEMENT TO ADDRESS ECOSYSTEM SERVICES

Watershed management and development refers to the conservation, regeneration and the judicious use of the natural (land, water, plants, and animals) and human habitat within a shared ecosystem (geological-hydrological-aquatic and ecological) located within a common drainage system. Over the years, watershed management has come to be seen as the initiation of rural development processes in arid and semi arid areas, in particular in rainfed ecosystems – combining projects for ecological sustainability with those for socio-economic development. Theoretically, it attempts to integrate sectors such as water management, agriculture, forestry, wasteland development, off-farm livelihood development, etc., and to establish a foundation for rural development. The approach aims to be flexible enough to be adapted to varying sociological, hydrological and ecological conditions (Joy *et al.*, 2006). Apart from the purely environmental concerns, i.e., restoring ecosystem functions, the watershed framework often focuses on livelihood improvements, poverty alleviation and a general increase in human well-being.

Watershed management is a strategy which responds to the challenges posed by a rainfed agro-ecosystem and human demands. Typically these challenges include water scarcity, rapid depletion of the ground water table and fragile ecosystems, land degradation due to soil erosion by wind and water, low rainwater use efficiency, high population pressure, acute fodder shortage and poor livestock productivity, mismanagement of water sources, and lack of assured and remunerative livelihood opportunities. Therefore, the watershed management approach seeks to ensure human well-being and progress toward sustainable development through improved ecosystem services—including food, fresh water, fuel wood, and fiber. Changes in availability of all these ecosystem services can profoundly affect aspects of human well-being — ranging from the rate of economic growth and level of health and livelihood security to the prevalence and persistence of poverty. The framework of watershed management acknowledges the dynamic interrelationship between people and ecosystems. To bring about a positive change in the ecosystem services of the local habitat, the watershed management approach deals with people and ecosystem in a holistic and inter-disciplinary way.

The water management component of watershed management in rainfed areas largely depends on rainwater to initiate the local development processes. Thus, the aim of this chapter is to highlight some of the critical issues facing rainwater harvesting in watershed management, against the backdrop of human and ecosystem well-being.

3.2 POTENTIAL OF RAINWATER HARVESTING IN WATERSHED ECOSYSTEM SERVICES AND HUMAN WELL-BEING

Watersheds consist of a complex pattern of various ecosystems (forests, farmland, wetlands, soils, etc) which provide a number of important goods and services for human well-being. Examples are ample and safe water supply from rivers and groundwater, crops, fish, fuel and fibres, as well as flood and erosion control. Rainwater is, by itself, an important input factor for healthy and productive ecosystems.

Rainwater harvesting in the context of a watershed means collecting runoff from within a watershed area, storing it, and employing it for different purposes. Runoff collection is generally distinguished as in situ management, when the water is collected within the area of harvesting, and *ex situ* when it is diverted outside of the harvesting area. The storage is of crucial importance: for in situ rainwater harvesting the soil acts as the storage, whereas for *ex situ* rainwater harvesting the reservoir can be natural or artificial, where natural generally means groundwater recharge, and artificial means surface/subsurface tanks and small dams. The differentiation between the two is often minor, as water collection structures are generally placed in a systematic relation with each other; hence, the runoff from certain structures may be a source of recharge for others. For example, the construction of anicuts (small dams) at frequent intervals in seasonal rivers leads to increased groundwater recharge. Rainwater harvesting in a watershed context has a role and an impact on several aspects of ecosystems and human well-being. This section will present a few of them, through examples and case studies.

Rainwater harvesting impacts on downstream flows?

Amongst the proponents of rainwater harvesting, the argument in favour of its potential to drought-proof India has developed so far as to prove that, if half of rainfall is captured, every village in India can meet its own domestic water needs (Agarwal, 2001). The strategy for drought proofing would be to ensure that every village captures all of the runoff from the rain falling over its entire land and the associated government revenue and forest lands, especially during years when the rainfall is normal, and stores it in tanks or ponds or uses it to recharge depleted groundwater reserves. It would then have enough water in its tanks or in its wells to cultivate

substantial lands with water-saving crops like millet and maize. Although detractors highlight the variability of rainfall and potential effect of heavy harvesting on downstream water resources during drought years, the resonance of this argument is strong. Rainfall can cover basic human needs in dry areas in a decentralized and sustainable way and thus reduce pressures on pressures of fragile groundwater reserves. These estimates prove that the potential of rainwater harvesting is large and that there is little reason why a village, region, or a country has to experience water problems, if they have land and rains. However, one of the conditions of sustainable watershed management is to recognise so-called negative externalities. In this case the negative externality would be the effects of rainwater harvesting on downstream water availability. Runoff out of the watershed may be considered as a waste from a local point of view, but it may be a key resource for surface withdrawals or recharge of groundwater for downstream users (Ruf, 2006). For example, the Sardar Patel Participatory Water Conservation programme was launched by the government of Gujarat in Saurashtra and north Gujarat in 1999, and involved the building of check dams in local streams, and nallas (drains). As the government of India officially claimed in 2007, nearly 54,000 check dams were built in Saurashtra and north Gujarat with the involvement of local communities. However, some caution has been raised, as this large and fast expansion of water harvesting potentially can affect the ecology of Saurashtra region (Kumar *et al.*, 2008).

Decentralized approach may give access to more water sources

Given the fact that rainfall is unevenly distributed between years, as well as within rainy seasons, storing rainwater is a key component of water management. The water can be stored in storages of different construction

Checkdam in village of Dotad Jhabua

Check dam   Prasad

and dimensions; for example, large reservoirs with large catchments and small tanks and ponds with small catchments, or use of natural or artificial groundwater recharge to store water in the soil.

There is evidence to show that village-scale rainwater harvesting will yield much more water for consumptive use than large or medium dams, making the latter a wasteful way of providing water, especially in dry areas. In the Negev desert where rainfall is only 105 mm annually, it was found that more water is collected if the land is broken up into many small catchments, as opposed to a single large catchment (Agarwal, 2001). This is because small watersheds provide an amount of harvested water per hectare which is much higher than that collected over large watersheds, as evaporation and loss of water from small puddles and depressions is avoided. As much as 75% of the water that could be collected in a small catchment is lost at the larger scale. It is important to recognize that the non-harvested water does not necessarily go to waste, as it is returned to the water cycle from the landscape (Ruf, 1998). Several other studies conducted by the Central Soil and Water Conservation Research Institute in Agra, Bellary and Kota, and another study conducted in the high rainfall region of Shillong, have all found that smaller watersheds yield higher amounts of water per hectare of catchment area. To put it simply, this means that in a drought-prone area where water is scarce, 10 tiny dams, each with a catchment of 1 ha, will collect

more water than one larger dam with a catchment of 10 ha. However, critics have suggested that the benefits of smaller rainwater harvesting systems versus large scale downstream implementation is mostly an effect of different scale and project implementation, and lack of consideration of (negative) externalities (Batchelor *et al.*, 2003). There is scientific evidence that even withdrawal of water by rainwater harvesting can have depleting effects, if the water is for consumptive uses such as irrigation. Evapotranspiration of plants (crops, trees, other vegetation) is an absolute loss of water, which potentially can affect downstream flows of water if used upstream excessively.

Increasing infiltration and groundwater recharge

Groundwater recharge in watershed management can be induced through different structures; for instance, through dug shallow wells and percolation tanks. The estimated number of dug shallow wells in varying formations and situations in Rajasthan is about 83,000 wells, with potential new nadis (village ponds) estimated at 14,500. The existing nadis and the ones to be built may contribute 360-680 million m^3 of groundwater replenishment annually. Percolation tanks alternatively are another recharge structure which is generally constructed on small streams and used for collecting the surface runoff. Under favorable hydro-geological conditions, percolation rates may be increased by constructing recharge (intake) wells within percolation tanks. According to studies conducted on artificial recharge, the percolation tanks constructed in hard rock and alluvial formations in the Pali district of Rajasthan had a percolation rate of 14 to 52 mm/day. Percolation accounted for 65-89% of the loss whereas the evaporation loss was only 11-35% of the stored water. The results also indicated that the tanks in a hard rock area contained water for 3-4 months after the receding of the monsoon. Percolation tanks have been of greater benefit in recharging groundwater in the neighboring Gujarat state. There is a huge potential to adopt this technology in western Rajasthan as well, where groundwater depletion rates are very high. Thus, percolation tanks hold great promise for drought mitigation in regions having impermeable strata beneath a sandy profile, with limited water holding capacity but high percolation rates.

However, the effectiveness of groundwater recharge in any area depends on the technical efficiency of recharging groundwater, the storage potential of the aquifers which are being recharged, and the dynamics of interaction between groundwater and surface water (Kumar *et al.*, 2008).

Reducing soil erosion

Rainfed areas are also confronted with problems of land degradation through soil erosion. Watershed management interventions through water harvesting are often synonymous with soil and water conservation. They act both to harvest rainfall and to conserve soil and water, as a mean of increasing farm productivity. The available evidence reveals that soil loss is reduced by about 0.82 tons per ha per year due to interventions in the watershed in India (Joshi *et al.*, 2005).

The consequence of these soil conservation activities also is the reduction of siltation of downstream tanks and reservoirs that in turn reduce the need for maintenance. An example is provided by a comprehensive assessment of the Rajasamadhiyala watershed, Gujarat, India, conducted to assess the on-site impact of a watershed management program as well as off-site impacts on two downstream watersheds. Inspection of the 40 year old check dam in the downstream portion of the Rajasamadhiyala watershed, showed that, two years after the check dams construction upstream, the check dam downstream was completely free from siltation whereas previously it had silted up every 2 years (Sreedevi *et al.*, 2006).

Intensification of crop production through rainwater harvesting

Reduction of surface runoff was used to augment both surface and shallow groundwater reserves through in situ rain water harvesting interventions. This had a direct benefit by expanding the irrigated area and increasing cropping intensity. On average, the irrigated area increased by 34%, while the cropping intensity increased by 64%. Such an impressive increase in the cropping intensity was not achieved in many surface irrigated areas in the country (Sreedevi *et al.*, 2006).

Action for Social Advancement's (ASA) work in Madhya Pradesh, India, provides an example of how the increased volume of rainfall infiltration and surface storage has resulted in additional irrigated area, contributing to increased crop output as well as cash crop production. The improved water availability in the soil, and irrigation supply, has enabled farmers to grow a second crop during the winter season, after the usual monsoon season (Table 3.1). The local cropping pattern has changed, and at present the farmers have started growing wheat during the winter, and rice and soybeans during the monsoon. As part of land development activities, several farmers have built small field bunds (in Hindi talais) to retain water in the fields that are flooded during the monsoon to grow a rice crop, for wheat production during the subsequent dry season.

Improving food security and economic security

Rainwater harvesting can be instrumental to decentralized water supplies and local food security. Local food security is as important as national food security. It has been proven that the overall increase in crop output, mainly from the second crop, and from the establishment of homestead (kitchen) gardens, has had an impact upon the amount of food available for domestic consumption (Joshi *et al.*, 2005). When rainwater harvesting at the household or community level enables rainfed farms to access a source of supplementary irrigation, the economic security also improves. According to farmers in the ASA implementation area in Madhya Pradesh (Pastakia, 2008), the visible signs of improved economic security are increased incomes

Crop irrigated through dug wells   Prasad

Dug wells recharged by in situ water harvesting

Prasad

from the sale of marketable agricultural surpluses, that typically has led to a reduction in dependency and debt, to a decrease in the reliance on moneylenders, and to an increase in savings and investment in new assets (primarily agriculture related assets) or improvement in existing assets.

As the ASA case study highlights, the household "hungry" period (related to a lack of food or funds) on average comprised 2-3 months, primarily from June-August. Currently, there is sufficient food for consumption either produced by the household itself or through a village level share arrangement. The second crop also has resulted in a significant financial saving to households through reduced staple food expenses and less debit repayment.

Additional potential impacts on human welfare

There are additional impacts of watershed management that may or may not have substantial effects on the overall outcomes.

The ASA case study provides an interesting example of positive synergies between improved social welfare and improved ecological benefits enabled by rainwater harvesting in watershed management. Migration is integral to the tribal lifestyle in Jhabua district, Madhya Pradesh, as during the summer months the adult male population migrates to Gujarat to become part of the construction labour force. However, an independent assessment has shown that the area within the watershed management project is currently witnessing a reduction in the migration of family members (primarily sons) and/or in the length of the migration period, due to guaranteed work, income and food security from enhanced agricultural production. The migration period has come down from 6-8 months to around 4 months.

Other effects relate to both social and ecological aspects of the watershed management interventions:

- Changes in food consumption habits, particularly the consumption of more vegetables; however, no in-depth assessment of the ramifications of this

Table 3.1: Change in typical cropping pattern, ASA , Madhya Pradesh

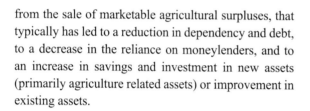

	Monsoon	**Winter**
Before irrigation source	maize, pigeon peas, lentils, groundnuts, black gram, sorghum	pigeon peas, maize, wheat
After irrigation source	rice, soybeans, maize, pigeon peas ,lentils, groundnuts	wheat, maize, pigeon peas, vegetables

(for instance on nutritional levels or incidence of malnutrition) has been carried out in the areas.

- Rainwater harvesting has the potential to mobilize and involve communities in securing access to water issues, building an effective structure can be a start for a process of self-management in village communities, if each step is the result of a cooperative social process that enhances the ability of a community to work in cooperation (Aarwal, 2001)

- Rainwater harvesting can help establish a culture of natural conservation and human synergetic existence in the environment amongst different sectors of the society

- Rainwater harvesting operates as an effective tool for addressing the problems of 'ecological poverty', as without water the process of ecological poverty cannot be reversed

- A decentralized water conservation and management system may help in ensuring local food security and substituting for external/centralized water supply mechanisms within a decentralized system that preserves local regulations

- Decentralised water supplies using rainwater harvesting technologies can lessen reliance on upstream land managers by downstream water users, both in terms of water quantity and/or quality

- Rainwater harvesting can serve to remediate impacts on environmental flows in natural rivers by contributing to sustainable flows during dry periods.

Specific attention should be given to the impact of rainwater harvesting and watershed management, or even water management in general, on gender issues. While the ASA case study presents a reflection on gender, there are very few assessments conducted over a long term, or after a few years from the implementation of the specific intervention of watershed management, assessing long-term impacts on both water flows and ecosystem services, as well as on the social, gender and economic impacts (Coles and Wallace, 2005).

3.3 CASE STUDIES WITH RAINWATER HARVESTING AS ENTRY POINT IN WATERSHED MANAGEMENT

Small river basin approach in watersheds, central west India

Action for Social Advancement (ASA) is a non-governmental organization based in Madhya Pradesh in Central West India (Appendix II: case 3.1). The organization's work focuses on improving the living environment and livelihood security of the local tribal communities. In 1996, ASA worked with 42 tribal villages (nearly 25,000 people) with a land area of nearly 20,000 hectares in Jobat, one of the sub-districts of Jhabua district in Madhya Pradesh, to carry out watershed work at the small river basin level. ASA was keen to adopt a river basin approach instead of using the conventional watershed strategy, because their previous experiences suggested that working on a few micro-watersheds within a river basin did not yield the expected outputs, as the micro-watershed interventions did not benefit of the greater basin water resources and ecosystem services.

In order to maximize the impact at the river basin level, ASA focused on the following activities:

- Land development It was considered fundamental for enhancing agricultural productivity to check the soil erosion and increase the infilration of rainfall

- Water resources development- With the intention of increasing the sub-surface and ground water flows and to ensure their continuity throughout the year by increasing the storage of surface water using rainwater harvesting structures, ASA implemented water storage, percolation tanks and masonry check dams

- Agriculture intensification and diversification – ASA worked on promoting appropriate farming technologies to the farmers and allowing farmers to test and adopt suitable technologies to build further on the regenerated resources. Diversification of crops (for instance, from cereal crop to vegetables or dry land horticulture) was another important strategy for optimizing farm productivity

- Build and promote people's institutions around the natural resource interventions, both in terms of water users' groups and watershed committees, as well as creating institutional mechanisms for the supply of agricultural credit.

The impact of ASA's watershed management at the river basin level can be assessed through its influence on human and ecosystem well-being. In general the subsurface flow of water has improved significantly, indicated by the increased flows in the streams and rivers in the entire basin. Hand pumps and dug wells have become permanent, while many of the dry dug-wells have been revived. Evidence of increased base flow can be confirmed by the fact that in last three years private investments have been directed towards shallow dug-wells.

Productivity has improved due to soil retention, double cropping, and reclamation of waste land. Agricultural extension has encouraged diversification of crops such as the introduction of improved varieties, vegetable cultivation, and small and medium drainage system converted into paddy fields. The net biomass at the household level has increased for consumption, for sale and for livesock. Significant income has been added to the farms through the implementation of dug wells, small group lift irrigation systems, orchards, vegetable gardens, and use of improved seeds and technologies like vermi composting. An unexpected positive trend is the reduced migration to cities, particularly in villages where the greatest work effort has been directed toward the areas land and water resources development. The increased access and institutional capacity of communities to manage agricultural credits has resulted in more opportunity for regular financial, insurance and agricultural service companies.

As yet, women's participation in the watershed management committees has been lacking. This has highlighted the need to integrate gender in the program. Currently the organization is at a crucial point in designing a framework to integrate strong and active SHGs (Self Help Groups) into the watershed management institutions.

Rainwater harvesting and urban water supply in the Giber basin,

Following significant population increases and housing standard improvements, Århus, Denmark's second largest city, was challenged by increased water demand and consumption (Appendix II: case 3.2). In the 1960s-early 1970s, this increased demand was met by pumping groundwater from the aquifers of the Giber basin, which soon resulted in negative impacts on the environmental flows and aquatic ecosystems in the area. First of all, the depletion of the groundwater was not matched by the natural recharge, making the pumping of water unsustainable. Secondly, as a consequence, the springs feeding the Giber basin, an ecosystem targeted for provision of recreational services, were running dry, particularly in the summer, when recreational use was high. Moreover, the low-flow discharge of the river consisted mainly of treated waste water discharges from the municipal treatment plants in the basin, with concomitant enrichment concerns. These impacts initiated considerable political concern, as the environmental movement was growing and the demand for recreational areas for use by the urban population became an important electoral issue.

Despite demand management enforcement, which was able to decrease the water use from 350 litres/day/person in 1970 to less than 200 litres/day/person in 2005, the authority realized that rainwater harvesting could be supportive in terms of maintaining the ecosystem and the related services it provides. In fact, the Giber basin contains several flood retention reservoirs, constructed in accordance with municipal regulations for storm water control, one of which was found to be feasible for storing rainwater for later controlled release, as a supplement to the natural flow.

To conclude, the mechanism for supporting the environmental flows in the Giber basin was found in rainwater harvesting through urban storm water management. With limited investment and a change in operational rules, the low flow of Giber basin could be supported by harvested rainwater. This simple and practical solution illustrates the potential of rainwater harvesting within a river basin as an area of cross-sectoral convergence (involving nature, urban stormwater management systems, and recreational use demands), within a basin, for human and ecosystem well-being. Specifically, the positive impacts of rainwater harbesting on the ecosystem were increased river flow in the landscape, supporting and regulating the related services of improved water quality, groundwater recharge and an increased water flow downstream and in springs.

The main impact of this intervention on human well-being has been through the support of the related environmental services, which was even made concrete by the inclusion of the basin in the EU network of protected areas NATURA2000 (Thomsen *et al.*, 2004)

The Karnataka Watershed development project: emerging negative externalities

The Karnataka Watershed Development Project (KAWAD) (Appendix II: case 3.3) is located in the northern districts of the Karnataka state in the south of India. The northern part of the state experiences water scarcity. To address this concern, KAWAD has been trying out different institutional mechanisms to identify the appropriate approach for resolving water use conflicts.

It is acknowledged that watershed management creates an enabling environment for human and ecosystem well-being, but occasionally it also is accompanied by new challenges caused by the watershed management interventions. According to the water resource audit of the KAWAD, enhanced water resources in the project areas have led to the intensification of demand and competition for water for competing human uses. Recently it was observed that the annual water use was as high as the annual replenishment of surface and groundwater resources and that there has been increasing conflict between the upstream and downstream water user groups.

In addition, the watershed has also attracted criticism due to its constricted and compartmentalized planning and execution policies and practices. For instance, after the implementation of KAWAD in the first half of 1999, it was realized that the importance and inclusion of water-related interventions, which mainly included check dams and other rainwater harvesting structures, was too exaggerated. These structures were inappropriate considering the surface flows in the region, which, prior to the watershed work, were already low. With the construction of the water harvesting structures, this flow was further reduced. The consequence was a new set of problems in the region, such as depleted groundwater levels, dry dug-wells, reduced domestic water supplies during the summer and the drought period. A shift in perspective from water development to water management, which included demand management and not only supply management, was a pre-requisite for developing a local modus operandi for achieving the desired watershed outcomes. Thus, although many watershed interventions have enabled development, water became the limiting resource and appropriate steps had to be taken for its sustainable and continuous use to support both improved human well-being and sustainable and productive ecosystem services.

3.4 CONCLUSION

Rainwater harvesting can be a vital intervention in the rehabilitation of ecosystem services for enhancing human well-being in the context of watershed management. Its appropriate application can influence changes in the well-being of both human-oriented and ecosystem services. The changes are triggered through synergies across sectors; for instance, through interactions between agricultural practices, rainwater recharge, soil conservation and food security needs. However, it is important to recognize that the approach of harvesting rainwater in watershed management, through major and minor schemes, has its own limitations, both in terms of appropriateness of the precise interventions, their techno-economic feasibility, and their practical method of implementation. Therefore, close monitoring of the impacts is required in environmental, economical, social and technical terms during all the phases of the project cycle as well as after the end of the project.

REFERENCES

AA.VV.2003. Water Harvesting and Management 2003, Practical guide series 6, Inter Cooperation and Swiss Agency for Development and Cooperation, New Delhi

Agarwal, A.2001. Drought? Try Capturing the Rain, Briefing paper for members of parliament and state legislatures, Occasional Paper, Centre for Science and Environment, New Delhi

Batchelor C.H., Rama Mohan Rao M.S., Manohar Rao S. 2003. Watershed development: A solution to part water storage in semi-arid India or part of the problem? Land Use and Water Resources Research Vol.3 2003 (1-10), Karnataka.

Coles A., Wallace T. 2005. Gender, Water and Development. Berg Publishers: Oxford

Dyhr-Nielsen, M. 2009. A tale of two cities: Meeting urban water demands through sustainable groundwater management. In: Robert Lenton *et al.*: IWRM in Practice, Earthscan, London, (in press).

Geddes J.C. 2007. Evaluation of ASA's Watershed Development work in selected villages in Jhabua district, Madhya Pradesh, Action for Social Advancement (ASA), Mumbai

Mondal Ashis. 2005. Small River Basin Approach in Watersheds in Central West India, Action for Social Advancement, Bhopal

Malviya, S., Gettings, S. 2007. Durable Livelihood Assets: Impact Assessment of ASA's Dug Wells Programme, Action for Social Advancement, Bhopal

Joshi, P. K.., Jha, A. K., Wani, S.P., Joshi, Laxmi, Shiyani, R. L. 2005. Meta-analysis to assess impact of watershed program and people's participation. Comprehensive Assessment Research Report 8. Colombo, Sri Lanka: Comprehensive Assessment Secretariat.

Joy K.J., Shah A., Paranjape S., Badiger S., Lele S. 2006. Reorienting the Watershed Development Programme in India, Occasional Paper, Forum for Watershed Research and Policy Dialogue

Kumar, M.D., Patel A., Ravindranath R., Singh O.P. 2008. Chasing a Mirage: Water Harvesting and Artificial Recharge in Naturally Water-Scarce Regions, in Economical and Political Weekly, August 30, 2008

Pastakia, A. 2008. Promotion of Micro finance initiatives in Jhabua district of Madhya Pradesh in central-west India, An Evaluation Study, Action for Social Advancement, Bhopal and Paul Hamlyn Foundation, UK

Ruf, T. 2006. La gestion participative de l'irrigation, compromis social ou précarité hydraulique ? Fausses apparences et vraies redistributions des pouvoirs sur les eaux en général et sur les eaux agricoles en particulier. Paper presented at "Colloque International Gevorev", UVSQ.

Ruf, T. 1998. "Du passage d'une gestion par l'offre en eau à une gestion par la demande sociale: Ordre et désordre dans les questions d'irrigation et de conflits d'usage de l'eau". Paper presented at "atelier 3 du IRD" November 1998. IRD, Montpellier

Sreedevi, T.K., Wani, S.P., Sudi, R., Patel, M.S., Jayesh, T., Singh S.N., Shah, T. 2006. On-site and Off-site Impact of Watershed Development: A Case Study of Rajasamadhiyala, Gujarat, India. Global Theme on Agroecosystems Report No. 20, Pantacheru, Andhra Pradesh, India: International Crops Research Institute for the Semi-Arid Tropics.

Thomsen, R., V.H. Søndergaard K.I Jørgensen. 2004. Hydrogeological mapping as a basis for establishing site-specific protection zones in Denmark. Hydrogeology Journal, Vol. 12, pp550-562

CHAPTER 4

RAINWATER HARVESTING IN THE MANAGEMENT OF AGRO-ECO SYSTEMS

Main author: Bharat Sharma, International Water Management Institute, New Delhi, India

Contributing authors:
Farai Madziva, Harvest Ltd, Athi River, Kenya.
Filbert B. Rwehumbiza, Siza Tumbo, S.D, Sokoine University of Agriculture, Tanzania
Mohamed Bouitfirass, National Institute of Agronomic research (INRA), SETTAT, Morocco
Mohamed Boufaroua. M, l'Aménagement et de la conservation des terres agricoles (ACTA), Tunis, Tunisie
Mohammed El Mourid, Centre International de Recherche Agricole dans les zones Sèches (ICARDA), Tunis, Tunisie
Adouba ould Salem, A. Projet de développement pastoral et de gestion de parcours (PADEL), République Islamique de Mauritanie

4.1 THE ROLE OF RAINFED FARMING FOR ECOSYSTEM SERVICES AND HUMAN WELL-BEING

Development of agriculture is the main landuse change that has affected and depleted many ecosystem services in favour of increased agricultural biomass production (MA, 2005). The soil and climate sets the parameters for agro-ecosystems. Increasingly, the value of a healthy soil system is recognised as a key ecosystem service in sustaining agro-ecosystem production. Water flows in the soil system depend upon two principal factors; infiltration of rainfall, and water holding capacity of the soil. Rainwater harvesting for crops is therefore closely related to soil system management; namely, the actions taken to improve infiltration into the soil and to increase water holding capacity and fertility functions in the soil.

In the water management community, much attention has been devoted to irrigated agriculture, since it appears to be the major consumer of water, when compared to water requirements for domestic and industrial purposes. However, much less attention has been paid by water managers and investment institutions to the issues of rainfed agriculture. The distinctive features of rainfed agriculture in developing countries are that both productivity improvement and expansion have been slower in relation to irrigated agriculture. But as Pretty and Hine (2001) suggest, there is a 100% yield increase potential in rainfed agriculture in developing countries, compared to only 10% for irrigated crops.

Rainfed agriculture produces, and will continue to produce, the bulk of the world's food. It is practised on 80% of the world's agricultural land area, and generates 65-70% of the world's staple foods, but it also produces the most food for poor communities in developing areas. In Sub-Saharan Africa more than 95% of the farmland is rainfed, while almost 90% in Latin America, 60% in South Asia, 65% in East Asia and 75% in the Near East and North Africa are rainfed. In India, 60% of water use in agriculture originates from directly infiltrated rainfall.

Low and variable productivity is the major cause of poverty for 70% of the world's poor inhabiting these lands. At the same time there is growing evidence that agriculture continues to play key role in economic development and poverty reduction in the rainfed regions. Increased effort is needed to upgrade rainfed systems, from the point of view of improving soil water capacity and fertility. More efficient rainwater harvesting systems have a great role to play, especially in developing countries struggling to provide water and affordable food.

Water security to ensure human well-being in rainfed farming systems

Yield gap analyses in tropical semi-arid and sub-humid areas found farmers' yield a factor of 2-4 times lower than optimally achievable yields, for major rainfed crops. Grain yields fluctuate around 1-2 t/ha, compared to optimal yields of over 4-5 t/ha (Falkenmark and Rockstrom, 2000). The large yield gap between attainable yields and farmers' practice, as well as between attainable and potential yields, shows that there is a large potential to improve yields in rainfed agriculture that remains to be tapped.

Rainfall is the crucial input factor in the rainfed production system. Its variation and uncertainty is high in areas of low rainfall and a major cause of low productivity and heightened distress among farmers. The last decade, in particular, has witnessed serious distress, even amongst the more enterprising, small and marginal farmers in the rainfed regions. They opted to replace traditional low value cereals with high value ones (but ones more vulnerable to dry spells and droughts), and introduce intensive crops through borrowing but with little success. Adverse meteorological conditions, long dry spells and droughts caused extended moisture stress periods for crops, livestock and people. Such situations occur over large parts of poor countries in Asia and sub-Saharan Africa. Limited food productivity and poverty at the household level is a major contributing factor in the further degradation of ecosystems, including deforestation, excessive abstraction of biomass, and possibly landscape habitat destruction, with biodiversity loss as a result. In particular, degraded soils with low productivity can send the relationship between the ecosystem and human well-being into a downward spiral, with diminishing yields, affecting farmers' livelihoods, and reduced capacity to restore and enhance the soil system's health to a more productive state.

Constraints of rainfed agriculture systems and role of rainwater harvesting

In the most arid zones (< 300 mm/annum), absolute water scarcity constitutes the major limiting factor in water provision. But in the vast semi-arid and dry sub-humid tropical regions, total seasonal rainfall is generally adequate to meet most needs and also to significantly improve agricultural water productivity, if it were evenly distributed. However, dry spells (or monsoon breaks), with little or no rainfall, occur in most cropping seasons during critical stages of plant growth. Soil moisture storage reaches critical limits and causes crop damage, or even failure. Most rural poor in Asia, Africa and Latin America experience water scarcity for agriculture, and consequentially poor yields and compromised livelihoods, due to the lack of public, private and individual investment in the provision of even small scale water infrastructure. Here adaptation to rainfall variability is the greatest water challenge.

Therefore, local harvesting of a small portion of the rainwater in wet periods, utilising the same for supplemental/protective irrigation during devastating dry spells, offers a promising solution in the fragile, rainfed regions of the world. As total rainfall is spread over a few rainfall events of high intensity (about 100 hours in whole season in semi-arid regions), in most rainfed regions in Asia and Africa much is lost to runoff and evapotranspiration. It is important to capture and convert a part of this into more productive use. The storm runoff may either be diverted directly and spread on the fields, or collected in inexpensive water storage systems.

Water harvesting techniques may be catchment systems, collecting runoff from a larger area. They include runoff farming, which involves collecting runoff from the hillsides and delivering it onto plain areas, and floodwater harvesting within a streambed using barriers (check dams) to divert stream flow onto an adjacent area, thus increasing infiltration of water into the soil. Micro-catchment water harvesting methods are those in which the catchment area and the cropped area are distinct, but adjacent to each other. Establishing catchment systems often necessitates ecosystem rehabilitation and conservation, in order to secure the runoff.

At the farm level, rooftop runoff collection may be successfully used for gardening. At the field level, in situ water harvesting methods focus on the storage capacity of the land surface and the soil. They include conservation tillage, field embankments, trenches, half-moon terraces and field terracing. Thus, the upper layers of the soil form an important part of the ecosystem, which act as a natural storage for rainfall. The infiltrated rainfall has an important role in supporting soil fertility cycles as well as micro-flora and fauna in the soil.

Generally, the amount of water made available through rainwater harvesting is limited and has to be used most judiciously to alleviate water stress during critical stages of crop growth. Supplemental irrigation is a key strategy, so far underutilised, in unlocking rainfed yield potentials. It is used on crops that can be grown using rainfall alone, but provides a limited amount of water during times of low/no rainfall. The use of supplemental irrigation, to bridge dry spells, has the potential to substantially increase yields by more than 100%. The existing evidence indicates that supplemental irrigation, ranging from 50-200 mm/season (500-2000 m3/ha), is sufficient to alleviate yield-reducing dry spells in most years, and thereby stabilise and optimise yield levels. In addition, supplemental irrigation systems have shown a further gain through improved water productivity; i.e., through gains in absolute consumption of water for the same production of biomass.

Rainwater harvesting serves as catalyst to improve farm ecosystem services and farm income

Existing research and farm-level and regional development programs aimed at improvement of the rainfed systems have shown that proper development and use of the water harvesting system is the first entry-point for success for most of these initiatives (Joshi et al., 2005; Rockstrom et al., 2007). The benefits associated with all additional activities concerned with improved soil and land management, such as crop and pest and disease management; investments in fertilizers, machinery and other agricultural investments; and development and access to markets, accrue to the field or the region which has a guaranteed access to the water resource.

Rainwater harvesting and its application to achieving higher crop yields encourages farmers to add value and diversify their enterprises. In parts of Tanzania, rainwater harvesting has enabled farmers in semi-arid areas to exploit rainfed farming by growing a marketable crop. Farmers upgraded from sorghum and millet to rice or maize, with additional legume crops that exploit residual moisture in the field. Similarly, studies of the Rajsamadhiyala watershed in Gujarat, India revealed that public investment in rainwater harvesting enabled farmers to invest in wells, pump sets, drip and sprinkler irrigation systems and fertilisers and pest management (Wani et al., 2006). In addition, farmers in the developed watershed villages in Andhra Pradesh, India allocated a greater area to vegetables and horticultural crops than did the farmers in the surrounding villages, which contributed to income stability and resilience. Farmers

also improved livestock and moved towards keeping large dairy animals (buffaloes, cows) rather than small grazing animals (sheep, goats) (Bouma et al., 2006). In this regard, the World Bank notes that each 1% growth in agricultural yield brings an estimated 0.5-0.7% reduction in rural poverty (World Bank, 2005) (Table 4.1). Thus water harvesting improves agricultural productivity with more value added outputs and boosts rural employment, both on and off the farm.

When on-farm productivity increases, thereby improving rural incomes and human well-being, other ecosystem services can improve too. This has been especially obvious where in situ rainwater harvesting has been implemented to reduce soil erosion. Increased farm productivity can reduce pressures on forestry and grazing, and thus increase habitats and biodiversity.

Introducing rainwater harvesting to improve soil ecosystem productivity in rainfed agriculture promises large social, economic, and environmental paybacks, particularly in poverty reduction and economic development. Rainwater harvesting presents a low-cost approach for mediating dry spell impacts in rainfed agriculture. Remarkable successes have in fact been witnessed in poverty- stricken and drought prone areas in India and Africa. In Sub-Saharan Africa, the future of over 90% rainfed farmers depends heavily on improved water security. In South Asia, about 70% of agriculture is rainfed and some good work has been done in the design and successful demonstration of a range of water harvesting structures, for both drinking water supply and irrigation. In several other countries in the Middle East, Latin America and South East Asia, rainwater harvesting is a traditional practice in certain regions, but the transferability of these models and practices has so far been limited. One of the main problems is that the local institutions needed often are inconsistent with the predominant governmental structures and institutional arrangements prevailing in these countries (Samra, 2005).

Investment in rainwater harvesting is important in meeting not only the Millennium Development Goals (Table 4.1) on reducing hunger but also on reducing poverty and ensuring environmental sustainability (Box-I, Sharma et al., 2008). A review of 311 case studies on watershed programs in India, with rainwater harvesting and rainwater management as important components, found that the mean cost-benefit ratio of

Table 4.1. Role of water harvesting in agriculture, in achieving the Millennium Development Goals (1, 3 and 7)

Millennium Development Goals(MDG)	Role of water harvesting in achieving the MDGs
Goal 1. Eradicate extreme poverty and hunger	There is a close correlation between hunger, poverty and water: most hungry and poor live in regions where water poses a particular constraint to food production. Water harvesting helps to mitigate the hunger-poverty-water nexus. (Rockstrom *et al.*, 2007)
a. Reduce by half the proportion of people living on less than a dollar a day.	a. Ca 75% of water required to achieve the 2015 MDG hunger reduction target will have to come from water investments in rainfed agriculture. (Molden , 2007)
b. Achieve full and productive employment and decent work for all, including women and young people.	b. Small investments (providing 1,000 m³ of extra water per hectare per season) in supplemental irrigation combined with improved agronomic practices can more than double yields and incomes in small-scale rainfed agriculture. Each 1% growth in agricultural yields brings about a 0.5%-0.7% reduction in the number of poor people. (World Bank, 2005)
c. Reduce by half the proportion of people who suffer from hunger.	Of the world's poor, 70% live in rural areas and are often at the mercy of rainfall-based sources of income. Upgrading rainwater management is a critical factor in increasing returns to labour and thus for poverty reduction. (Hatibu *et al.*, 2006; Sharma et al., 2008)
Goal 3. Promote gender equality and empower women	Increased efforts to promote home gardens, growing of vegetable and horticultural crops and improved livestock and poultry management through rainwater harvesting contribute to income stability which benefits women and children. Diversified livelihood options for women and youth increase resilience during drought years. (Joshi *et al.*, 2005; Sreedevi *et al.*, 2006). It also provides better nutrition for women and children.
Goal 7. Ensure environmental sustainability	Upgrading rainfed agriculture has substantial payoffs for society. Rainwater harvesting based watershed programs generated large on-and off-farm employment opportunities, and conserved soil and water resources (Sharma *et al.*, 2005).
a. Reduce biodiversity loss, achieving by 2010, and a significant reduction in the rate of loss.	Improved rainfed agriculture reduces the pressure on forests, grazing lands, wetlands and other fragile ecosystems and helps to improve biodiversity. Better use of green water improves biodiversity on 80% of the land area (Bruce *et al.*, 1999).
b. Reduce by half the proportion of people without sustainable access to safe drinking water and sanitation.	Rain water harvesting structures, especially based on rooftop rainwater harvesting is the most economical and surest way of providing water for drinking and sanitation even in the remotest areas. With small additional investment its safe use can be ensured (van Koppen *et al.*, 2008).

such watershed programs was relatively high at 1:2.14 (Joshi *et al*., 2005). Rain water harvesting created new/additional sources of water and helped in the provision and regulation of the water supply systems. Poor management of rainwater in rainfed systems generates excessive runoff and floods, causing soil erosion and poor yields. Investment that maximises rainwater harvesting, both in situ and *ex situ*, helps to minimise land degradation, while increasing the water available for productive use. Investment is now needed in water resource management, in smallholder rainfed farming systems, which adds additional freshwater and improved soil storage capacity and productivity. A small investment (providing 50 to 200 mm of extra water per hectare per season) for supplemental irrigation, in combination with improved agronomic management, can more than double water productivity and yields in small-scale rainfed agriculture. This will release pressure on surface water or ground water for irrigation. It will make more water available to sustain aquatic ecosystems, without compromising agricultural productivity. Increased rainwater infiltration can also artificially recharge the depleted groundwater aquifers in hard rock regions and in areas of intensive groundwater use. Governments in India and Pakistan have developed elaborate master plans for the artificial recharge of the aquifers through recharge wells, recharge shafts and recharge ponds (Romani, 2005; Shah, 2008).

However, as also elaborated in Chapter 3, environmental and social concerns need to be given due consideration when implementing rain water harvesting projects. In basins with limited surplus supplies, rainwater harvesting in the upstream areas may have a damaging impact downstream and can cause serious community conflict. Also, when runoff is generated from a large area and concentrated in small storage structures, there is a potential danger of water quality degradation, through introduction of agro-chemicals and other impurities. Special investigations on water quality must be undertaken before using the harvested water for recharge of underground aquifers.

4.2. GLIMMERS OF HOPE: CASE STUDIES OF RAINWATER HARVESTING

Several government and private institutions, civil society organisations and even committed individuals, in different parts of the developing world, have demonstrated the impressive benefits of rainwater

harvesting in improving agriculture, environment and human livelihoods. Some case studies, mentioned below, illustrate innovative structures for the provision and regulation of water-related ecosystem services, development of effective institutions and policies, establishment of new ways of inclusive development, improvement of degraded environments and securing of livelihood benefits for individuals and communities. Certain negative impacts on human well-being and ecosystem services, mentioned in the case studies and accompanying appendices, should also receive due consideration when considering new rainwater harvesting programs.

"Sukhomajri" – harvesting catchment runoff for the benefit of rural ecosystems and the welfare of rural populations

Sukhomajri is a small hamlet (59 families in the 1975, and 89 in the 1990, census surveys) with average land holdings of 0.57 ha, located in the Shiwalik foothills, India. In 1975, the village was completely rainfed and had no external sources of water for domestic use, livestock watering and crop irrigation. Yields were low and crop failures were common. Agriculture did not provide adequate livelihood support for the people. Illicit cutting of trees and uncontrolled grazing resulted in rapid denudation and erosion of hill slopes (80t/ha/year) which also seriously threatened the nearby lake. An integrated watershed development programme, with a major emphasis on rain water harvesting, was then planned. The area was treated with a series of staggered contour trenches on vulnerable slopes; stone, earthen and brushwood check dams in gullies; and graded stabilisers in the channels. A six metre high earthen embankment pond with 1.8 ha-m storage to harvest rainwater from a 4.2 ha catchment was constructed in 1976. Crop yields were doubled as a result of the use of supplementary irrigation water and improved land management practises. Livestock water needs and domestic water requirements were satisfied for all the households.

This gave impetus to a watershed management programme for the mutual benefit of the catchment and the command area, in which it was possible to combine the interests of the people with the improvement of the hilly catchment ecosystems. As a result of these interventions, vegetation began to appear in the catchment area and soil erosion was reduced by 98%, to about 1 t/ha/ year in a 5-year period. Later on, the

Box 4.I: Rainwater harvesting realising the potential of rainfed agriculture in India

India ranks first among the rainfed agricultural countries in terms of both extent (86 M ha) and value of produce. The traditional subsistence farming systems have changed and presently farmers have limited options. Farmers have started cultivating high value crops which require intensive use of inputs, most importantly life saving irrigation. Frequent occurrence of mid-season and terminal droughts of 1 to 3-weeks consecutive duration during the main cropping season are the dominant reasons for crop (and investment) failures and low yields. Provision of critical irrigation during this period has the potential to improve the yields by 29 to 114 per cent for different crops. A detailed district and agro-ecoregional level study, comprising 604 districts, showed that on a potential (excluding very arid and wet areas) rainfed cropped area of 25 M ha, a rainfall surplus of 9.97 M ha-m was available for harvesting. A small part of this water (about 18%) was adequate to pro-

vide one critical irrigation application of 18.75 M ha during a drought year and 22.75 M ha during a normal year. Water used in supplemental irrigation had the highest marginal productivity and increases in rainfed production above 50% were achievable. More specifically, net benefits improved by about 3-times for rice, 4-times for pulses and 6-times for oilseeds. Droughts appear to have limited impact when farmers are equipped with rainwater harvesting systems. Water harvesting and supplemental irrigation was economically viable at the national level and would have limited impacts downstream during normal years. This decentralized and more equitable intervention targeted resource poor farmers and has the potential to serve as an alternative strategy to the proposed river linking and water transfer projects.

Source: Sharma *et al.* (2008)

people themselves started protecting the forest and the grazing land, and the concept of 'Social Fencing' came into existence. However, it was soon realized that one check dam was insufficient to meet the needs of the village. In the following years, three additional water harvesting earthen dams were constructed. These ponds were sufficient to carry over the rainy season water for the winter crops and produce good yields. Even during drought years (when the crops of the adjoining villages did not produce any marketable yield) the stored water was sufficient to provide one/two irrigations, and meet the domestic and livestock water needs.

The demonstration of irrigating fields with stored runoff generated a tremendous enthusiasm among farmers. This introduced a new concept of watershed management for the mutual benefit of the catchment and the command area. Additionally, erosion and sediment delivery from the catchment were considerably reduced. This had been a major source of degradation and pollution to the adjoining 'Sukhna Lake'- a source of water supply and recreation for the neighbouring state capital city of Chandigarh. The entire management of the project was handed over to a new village based institution - the "Hill Resource Management Society" (HRMS). The Sukhomajri project indicated that people's participation had to be integrated into the planning and implementation

of the project. Even after thirty years since the initial rain water harvesting and additional interventions, the village continues to meet its domestic and productive water needs, has rejuvenated the grasslands, and enjoys much improved livelihoods through higher economic benefits (Arya and Samra, 2001).

Rainwater harvesting for commercial floriculture: Athi River Town, Kenya

The horticultural farm (commercial rose cultivation) of Harvest Ltd. is situated along the banks of the Athi River outside Nairobi, Kenya (Appendix II, Case 4.2). The Athi is a perennial river but within the project area it flows only for 5 months (January, February, March, November and December).

Athi River Town and its catchment area have a bimodal rainfall pattern. For the last 6 years the average rainfall of 800 mm has dropped to an average of 500 mm. Such a significant drop (40%) directly affects food production and the availability of clean water. Due to the proximity to the Athi catchment plains, there are high sodium (Na) levels in the soils and underground water. The groundwater has sodium levels as high as 450 ppm. The combination of poor soil quality and high sodium makes growing flowers in such soils challenging. A clean source of water was necessary for any sustainable crop

Rainwater harvesting and conveyance in stone and concrete drains   F Madziva

production to take place. The solution was rainwater harvesting, storage and usage. Harvest Ltd. invested in water storage facilities to ensure that all rain water was collected and stored safely. In total, Harvest Ltd. requires on average about 300,000 m^3 of water for irrigation per year for the 30 ha farm. Rainwater harvesting contributes 60% of this total water requirement. The harvested water reduces demand on other water extractions in the landscape. It uses three types of rainwater harvesting techniques; namely, rooftop, surface runoff and flood flow water harvesting. 95% of all rooftop catchment water is collected into reservoir.

Surface runoff is also collected in storm-drains and stored in reservoirs. Flood flow water is pumped out from the Athi River. This however, is not rainwater harvesting and has serious consequences downstream. Harvest Ltd. is able to pump these flood waters into reservoirs for storage for use during the dry periods. There are two big compacted earthen reservoirs having a maximum capacity of 230,000 cubic meters.

Rainwater harvesting reservoir at 90% capacity at Harvest Ltd., Athi River Town   F Madziva

The reservoirs can hold the water for a whole season without losing much to percolation. Rainwater harvesting and its storage would be an effective solution for both commercial and subsistence farmers. If it were not for rainwater harvesting, storage and good usage, Harvest Ltd. would have had to sink four extra boreholes to efficiently irrigate the 30 hectares of roses. By utilizing rainwater, pressure is released on the landscape water resources, as well as on groundwater for ecosystem and human uses.

Photo (left): Athi River - Dry (September 2006)
Photo (right): Athi River- Flowing (October 2008)   F Madziva

Water harvesting for livestock: 'charco dams' at South Pare Mountains, Tanzania

Livestock are an essential part of many smallhold, (semi-) subsistence farming systems. However, livestock also need to consume large amounts of fresh water. The case study of charco dams for livestock watering is based in the area below the South Pare Mountains of Tanzania (Appendix II: Case 4.4). The area covers over 700 km² and has a population of 35,000, with close to 200,000 head of cattle, with most of them located in the lowlands. The climate in the lowlands is semi-arid, with annual rainfalls of less than 500 mm, distributed over two seasons. The main economic activities are livestock rearing and crop production. Crop production without supplemental rainwater harvesting is practically impossible. The piped supply does not meet domestic water needs. Keeping livestock is thus a big challenge in the absence of drinking water. Pastoralists (mainly Pare and Masaai tribes) are normally forced to move animals to areas close to River Pangani in search of water and pastures during the dry season. The adoption of 'charco dams' in the past 15 years has partially reduced the crisis of availability of water for livestock in the area. Most pastoralists with more than 30 head of cattle own at least one charco dam for storage of water, required during the dry season.

A charco dam has three components: a runoff generating or collection area, in this case, the rangelands; a conveyance system made up of a network of shallow canals (up to 2 km); and a storage area (excavated pond). Thorny brush wood planted around the dam serves as a barrier to control access to the water. Recent additions include livestock drinking troughs, into which water is pumped from the pond using a treadle or motorized pumps, and a storage tank above ground. Although water is primarily for livestock watering, it is used also for domestic purposes and homestead vegetable gardens. Water stored in a charco dam lasts for 2 – 6 months (SWMRG, 2001).

Guaranteed access by the poor livestock farmers and their families to water resources had a positive impact on human well-being and the provision of ecosystem services. The health of farmers, women and children, and even livestock, improved due to enhanced water supplies that met their drinking and domestic water needs. The incomes of the farmers increased as better marketing opportunities for the livestock products, meat and milk appeared. With lactating animals being kept close to the homestead, women were easily able to market the milk, and thus access this source of income which was previously unavailable. Additionally, women no longer had to walk long distances in search of water required for domestic chores. The charco dams have also improved the ecosystems by reducing the pressure of animals on grasslands during the dry periods, creating water bodies dotted over the landscape, and improving growth of agriculture crops and other forms of vegetation. The mortality rate of lactating and young cattle has declined and families have better access to nutrition and sanitation.

Livestock drinking trough and storage tank beside the charco dam   S Tumbo

Photo (left): Silt trap intercepts sediments from the rainwater   S Tumbo

Farmer and environmental benefits of rainwater harvesting in Sekkouma –Irzaine, Morrocco and Kiffa, Mauretania

In the Mediterranean arid zone of Morocco, a range of in situ and *ex situ* rainwater harvesting interventions have been implemented to increase low-yielding farming systems and inadequate domestic water supply in the Sekkouma-Irzaine (Appendix II: Case 4.4). The area covers 87,000 km² with a population of ca 7,500 smallholder farmers in pastoralist communities. Primarily, rain water harvesting aimed to improve on-farm productivity and household water accessibility, but it turned out to have multiple positive benefits for the ecosystem as well. Implementation had a positive effect on the local community, in particular on women and children, who now had their time and effort previously devoted to fetching water reduced as a result of the household tanks. Social capital was built through the community organisation needed to implement the different in- and *ex situ* rain water harvesting systems. The gains from increased farm production improved both nutritional status in the households, and also household incomes, as the surplus of farm produce, both crops and livestock, is sold. The ecosystem services also were positively affected. Implementation of in situ water harvesting (banks, terraces, contour ridges, etc) increased soil infiltration thereby providing more soil moisture, which enabled better vegetative growth; i.e., improved provisional capacity. More species could thrive both on- and off-farm. In particular trees, shrubs and other permanent vegetation increased as an effect of the rainwater harvesting structures. Two key regulatory services improved in addition; firstly, soil erosion was reduced, and, secondly, lower lying villages were less affected by seasonal flooding events. The 'greening' of the landscape with more trees and water features improved the aesthetic aspect of the community.

A similar story emerges from Kiffa, in the Sahelian part of Mauretania (Appendix II: Case 4.5). As in Sekkouma-Irzaine, annual rainfall is around 300 mm but with extremely high temperatures, creating an arid environment. Approximately 1,200 inhabitants live and use the area of 17 km² for pastoral production and extensive cropping. Droughts and dry spells are the norm, challenging every effort to invest in, and improve, the current farming systems. In addition, the sandy soils are very prone to wind and water erosion, partly as a result of sparse vegetation cover. Through an initiative between the local community, local government and ICARDA, several in situ and *ex situ* rainwater harvesting interventions were carried out in the area. The primary target was to improve domestic water supply and on-farm water access for crops and livestock. These aims were achieved, and several additional positive effects materialised. Through the rainwater harvesting interventions and the follow-on effects on farming, jobs were created in the area. The interventions also created better community coherence and improved internal communication. Through a small dam (45,000 m3), 6ha of crop land could be irrigated. Runoff strips added another 2.5 ha to irrigated production. Increased vegetation cover and species diversification are additional positive impacts of the rainwater harvesting interventions. Water points for livestock and recharging of shallow wells were further gains. The regulatory services improved as well. In particular, soil loss decreased through the trapping of sediments in the in situ water harvesting structures, and incidences of flooding decreased in lower lying villages. Thus, in Sekkouma-Irzaine and in Kiffa, rainwater harvesting with water resource management has created positive synergies between the improvement in human well-being and regeneration of ecosystems in an extremely fragile environment.

4.3 CONCLUSIONS AND KEY MESSAGES

The soil is a key part of the agro-ecosystem, which with proper management, provides goods and services in the form of crops and erosion control. Upper layers of the soil are thus an important part of the ecosystem for harvesting, retention and storage of water supplies. Water security – in particular of rainwater – is a key factor in maintaining the goods and services provided by soils. This applies in particular to rainfed agriculture. Low and variable productivity in rainfed agricultural areas is the major cause of poverty of 70% of the world's poor.

Local harvesting of a small portion of the rainwater through in situ conservation practices and *ex situ* water harvesting structures provides great opportunities for sustaining farm ecosystems and their crops and livestock benefits. Utilisation of this resource for supplemental/ protective irrigation of farm crops, developing small homestead gardens or even large commercial production facilities and meeting livestock water needs to mitigate the impacts of devastating dry spells, offers a real opportunity to increase productivity in the fragile rainfed regions of the world. Furthermore, a secure water resource encourages farmers to add value and diversify their enterprises through the inclusion of vegetable and horticultural crops, improving livestock by moving towards the rearing of large dairy animals. This in turn leads to more value-added outputs and growth in rural employment, both on and off the farm. Strong evidence supports the view that proper development and use of the water harvesting system is the first entry point for success of the farm-level, or regional, development programs, in rainfed areas.

Investment in rainwater harvesting is important for meeting not only the Millennium Development Goals on reducing hunger, but also on reducing poverty and ensuring environmental sustainability. In particular, rainwater harvesting in watershed management may serve as an important incentive to protect woodlands and to reduce vulnerability of lands and water resources to erosion and sediment load deposition. Also, most water harvesting systems have a favourable mean cost-benefit ratio.

REFERENCES

Arya, S.L., Samra, J.S. 2001. Revisiting watershed management institutions in Haryana Shivaliks, India. Central soil and Water Conservation Research and Training Institute, Chandigarh, India, pp. 329.

Bouma, J., Soest, D., Bulte, E.H. 2005. Participatory watershed development in India: A sustainable approach. In. Sharma, B.R, Samra, J.S., Scott, C.A., Wani, S.P. (Eds.). 2005. Watershed Management Challenges: Improving productivity, resources and livelihoods. International Water Management Institute, Colombo, Sri Lanka.

Bruce, J.P., Frome, M., Haites, E., Janzen, H., Lal, R. Paustian, K. 1999. Carbon sequestration in soils. J. Soil and Water Conservation, 54(1): 283-289.

Falkenmark, M., Rockstrom, J. 1993. Curbing rural exodus from tropical drylands. Ambio 22(7): 427-437.

Falkenmark, M., Fox, P., Persson, G., Rockstrom, J.2001.Water Harvesting for Upgrading of Rainfed Agriculture: Problem Analysis and Research Needs. Stockholm International Water Institute, Stockholm, Sweden,

Hatibu, N., K. Mutabzi, E.M. Senkondo, A.S.K. Msangi. 2006. Economics of rainwater harvesting for crop enterprises in semi-arid areas of East Africa. Agricultural Water Management 80(3): 74-86.

Joshi, P.K., A. K. Jha, .S.P. Wani, Laxmi Joshi, RL Shiyani. 2005. Meta analysis to assess impact of watershed program and people's action. Comprehensive Assessment Research Report 8, International Water Management Institute, Colombo.

Molden, David (eds.).2007. Water for Food, Water for Life: A Comprehensive Assessment of Water Management in Agriculture. London: Earthscan, and Colombo: International Water Management Institute Pretty, J, R. Hine. 2001. Reducing Food Poverty with Sustainable Agriculture: A Summary of New Evidence. Final report of the "Safe World" Research Report. University of Essex, UK.

Rockstrom, J., Falkenmark, M. 2000. Semi-arid crop production from a hydrological perspective- Gap between potential and actual yields. Critical Reviews in Plant Sciences, 19(4): 319-346

Rockstrom, J., N. Hatibu, T.Y. Oweis, S.P. Wani, J. Barron, A. Bruggeman, J. Farahani, L. Karlsberg, Z. Qiang. 2007. Managing Water in Rainfed Agriculture. In. Molden, D. (Eds.). Water for Food, Water for Life: A Comprehensive Assessment of Water Management in Agriculture. London: Earthscan, and Colombo:

International Water Management Institute. Pp. 315-352.

Romani, S. 2006. National blueprint for recharging groundwater resources in India. In. Sharma, B.R., Villholth, K.G., Sharma, K.D. (Eds.) Groundwater research and management: Integrating science into management decisions. International Water Management Institute, Colombo, Sri Lanka, pp. 75-86.

Samra, J.S. 2005. Policy and institutional processes of participatory watershed management in India: Past lessons learnt and future strategies. In. Sharma, B.R.; Samra, J.S.; Scott, C.A.; Wani, S.P.(eds.).2005. Watershed Management Challenges: Improving productivity, resources and livelihoods. International Water Management Institute, Colombo, Sri Lanka. pp.116-128.

Shah, T. 2008. India's masterplan for groundwater recharge: an assessment and some suggestions for revision. Economic and Political Weekly (India) 43(51): 41-49.

Sharma, B. R., K. V. Rao, K. P. R. Vittal, U. Amarasinghe. 2008. Converting rain into grain: Opportunities for realising the potential rainfed agriculture in India. Proceedings National Workshop of National River Linking Project of India, International Water Management Institute, Colombo (pp. 239-252) available at http://www.iwmi.cgiar.org/Publications/ Other/PDF/NRLP%20Proceeding-2%20Paper%20 10.pdf

Soil-Water Management Research Group (SWMRG). 2001. Improving Water Availability for Livestock in Northern Tanzania through Rainwater Harvesting. Critical Problems facing Charcos, proposed intervention measures and requested assistance. Sokoine University of Agriculture, Tanzania, 5 pp.

Sreedevi, T.K., S.P. Wani, R. Sudi, M.S. Patel, T.Jayesh, S.N. Singh , T.Shah. 2006. On-site and Off-site impacts of watershed development: A case study of Rajasamdhiyala, Gujarat, India. Global theme on Agroecosystems Report 20. Andhra Pradesh, India: International Crops Institute for the Semi-Arid Tropics.

Van Koppen, B., R.Namara, C. C. Stafilos-Rothschild. 2005. Reducing poverty through investments in agricultural water Management: Poverty and gender issues and synthesis of Sub-Saharan Africa Case study Reports. Working paper 101. International Water Management Institute, Colombo.

Wani, S.P., Y.S. Ramakrishna, T.K.Sreedevi, T.D.long, T.Wangkahart, B.Shiferaw, P.Pathak, A.V.R. Kesava Rao. 2006. Issues, concepts, approaches and practices in integrated watershed management: Experience and lessons from Asia. In. B. Shiferaw and K.P.C. Rao (eds.) Integrated management of watersheds for agricultural diversification and sustainable livelihoods in eastern and central Africa: Lessons and experiences from semi-arid South Asia, International Crops Research Institute for the Semi-Arid Tropics, Patancheru, India

World Bank. 2005. Agricultural Growth for the Poor: an agenda for development. Washington, D.C.: World Bank.

CHAPTER 5

FORESTS WORKING AS RAINWATER HARVESTING SYSTEMS

Main author: Anders Malmer, Swedish University of Agricultural Sciences (SLU), Umeå, Sweden

Contributing authors:
Ulrik Ilstedt, Swedish University of Agricultural Sciences (SLU), Umeå, Sweden
Jennie Barron, Stockholm Environment Institute, York, UK/Stockholm Resilience Centre, Stockholm, Sweden

5.1. GLOBAL TRENDS IN FOREST COVER

Net deforestation has lost some pace during the last decades, but is still severe in a global context (FAO, 2005). Notably, the range and nature of deforestation is very variable in different regions and countries. In many cases, with intensifying cultivation and conversion to pasture or permanent low-input agriculture, the result is not only loss of biodiversity and its related ecosystem services, but landscapes are at risk of erosion, water pollution, flooding and decreasing soil productivity. These land use and land quality developments are very undesirable from the perspective of meeting the needs for increased biomass production for food and energy, as well as for ensuring a supply of clean water. On the other hand, much less attention is given in the media to the simultaneous processes of increasing forested areas in some regions and the increasing use of planted trees for various purposes. Planted forests have historically contributed to development in many countries in temperate regions, and have the potential to improve the livelihoods of millions of people in other regions. Today, planted forests comprise 6.9% of the world's total forest area of which more than half is located in the South. In 2050, FAO predict that 75% of global wood consumption will come from planted forests and that this expansion will be global. Recent expectations of forests as bio-energy reserves may dramatically raise the demands for new planted forests. 75% of planted forests are intended for industrial production. Forests owned by smallholders increased more than 3 times during 1990-2005 and now represent over 30% of all planted forests (FAO, 2005; 2006). Outside these figures, trees planted outside forests and on homesteads are increasing steadily. Apart from FAO definitions of planted forests (Table 5.1), this group represents a continuum of use of trees for a variety of purposes in small woodlots, agroforestry and homesteads. Most of the small holder increase is in Asia. In Africa there is a significant increase in timber plantations. In the near and mid-term future, these plantations will continue to expand, driven primarily by the growing demand from China and India. In recent years, both countries have invested heavily in timber plantation holdings, both nationally and overseas.

Agroforestry, or systems of intercropping permanent and annual crops, has gained a positive aura and developed strongly to improve traditional cultivation systems in a broad variety of environments. The relative success of biomass production in planted forestry has in many cases been overshadowed by negative ecosystems impacts and social-institutional issues. Ecosystem services affected include shifts of water use within the landscape and losses of biodiversity when converting from natural forest. When established without consideration of local stakeholders exclusion from previous livelihoods, it has sometimes caused longstanding conflicts. However, as the natural forest cover continues to degrade and decrease, there is an increasing need for planted forests. In the case of smallholders, crop and land tenure policies often do not favour investments by farmers on land out of their control. Improved management and tenure systems are needed for safeguarding the social and environmental values of forests in the entire landscape. This chapter will discuss the link between forests, water and ecosystem services for human well-being. It will provide an introduction to the potentially high values of establishing stable planted forests for "rain water harvesting" as one potential intervention to rehabilitate

Table 5.1: Definitions of planted forest in the forest continuum from natural forests to single trees.

FAO, 2007

Naturally regenerated forests		Semi-natural		Plantations		Trees outside forests
			Planted forests			
Primary	Modified natural	Assisted natural regeneration	Planted component	Productive	Protective	
Forest of native species, where there are no clearly visible indications of human activities and the ecological processes are not significantly disturbed	Forest of naturally regenerated native species where there are clearly visible indications of human activities.	Silvicultural practices by intensive management: •Weeding •Fertilizing •Thinning •Selective logging	Forest of native species established through planting or seeding, intensively managed	Forest of introduced and/or native species established through planting or seeding mainly for production of wood or non-wood goods	Forest of introduced and/or native species established through planting or seeding mainly for provision of services	Stands smaller than 0.5 ha; tree cover in agricultural land (agroforestry systems, home gardens, orchards); trees in urban environments; and scattered along roads and in landscapes

landscapes, giving examples from tropical semi-arid and humid cases. Also we would like to emphasis the need for development of more varied plantation practices and better understanding of the water-related values of planted forests in the wide range of settings where they are used.

Forests, trees and bushes form specific part of landuse systems. Considering the water balance, tress normally uses more water per area than an annual cereal crop in the very same location. Thus, the 'old paradigm' of forests as 'water towers' or as 'water protectors' is rarely valid in the landscape (Jackson *et al.*, 2005). However, the provisional ecosystem services capacity of a woodlot, apart from water, can outweigh those of the same area being cultivated. In general, the total biomass gain is higher and biodiversity is improved, provisioning a range of produce which can be harvested, often more reliably than annual crop systems. Forests also provide wood and energy. From a regulatory perspective, trees and forests play a significant role in affecting soil infiltration capacity and reducing erosion. They enhance soil quality through litter fall and extensive root systems, and have been shown to act as water purifiers. Trees and forests in many cultures often fall under special local management systems, to ensure their sustainable maintenance. Often, trees and forests are associated with high aesthetic and spiritual values. Thus, from a comprehensive livelihood perspective, forests and trees in the landscape offers multiple ecosystem services for the water consumed. Many of these products are essential in times of crop failure, when forest products can provide food and income in times of crisis.

5.2 FORESTS ECOSYSTEMS AS WATER HARVEST INTERVENTIONS FOR HUMAN WELFARE

It is now an empirically and theoretically well-established general scientific paradigm that forests use more water than lower vegetation and annual crops in rainfed agriculture. Consequently, empirical evidence is strong that cutting forests results in increased stream flows (Bosch and Hewlett, 1982). Typically, when forest cover is regenerated, more rainfall tends to (once again) be partitioned through soil infiltration and to green water (used for food and fibre production), reducing its availability as blue water (available for human consumption) downstream (Farley *et al.*, 2005; Scott *et al.*, 2005).

As a special case in semi-arid areas, old growth forests may work as "sponges" to better retain or recharge groundwater and to maintain dry season stream flow.

This has long been an item for scientific and policy debate (Bruijnzeel, 2004). Forests have been shown to maintain a high soil infiltration capacity by superior litter fall and soil protection (e.g., Bruijnzeel, 1990). Increasing surface runoff after deforestation increases surface run-off and possible soil deterioration, leading to more "blue water," but water that is often polluted by soil erosion. The higher surface runoff during rainfall events at a deforested location means that less water is contributed to long term groundwater recharge on site during the wet season. Depending on the location, shallow groundwater is often linked to lower lying stream flows, regulating the river base flow during dry seasons. Decreasing shallow groundwater recharge through deforestation may thus deplete surface water sources in times of high demand. The reduction of stream flow after deforestation has often been observed by rural people, but only a few studies have reported the expected long term decline in dry season flows (Bruijnzeel, 1989; Sandström, 1998). Thus, we have some evidence that a "sponge effect" can be lost by deforestation and subsequent soil degradation, but the conclusion can hardly be made general for all semi-arid forest ecosystems.

Based upon evidence on how tree litterfall and soil protection can improve soil quality and reduce surface runoff and erosion (e.g. Hurni and Tato, 1992), the restoration of a "forest sponge effect" has generally been taken for granted (Kaimowitz, 2005). This has been the paradigm behind numerous forest/tree planting projects and one of several drivers for adoption of agroforestry. However, in this case, there are many local witnesses to the fact that new forests often make wells and streams even drier than after deforestation. As for scientific studies in this case, long term studies are scarce. In contrast to the "lost sponge effect" paradigm, the few studies conducted in semi-arid environments all confirm that new forests use more green water than they contribute to blue water in terms of groundwater recharge. This effect of "not enough ground water recharge" is manifested in these studies as generally declining stream flows following (re)forestation (Scott et al., 2005).

High water use by new forests reflects higher production. The new forests established are most often planted exotic species like eucalyptus and pines. They are chosen for their high productivity. Many of the species used are pioneer species in their respective original ecosystems, and increasingly they are genetically improved for fast wood production, but not necessarily to be water efficient. Furthermore, these new forests are monocultures of vigorously growing young trees in contrast to old growth forest, which are mixes of species, old trees, young trees and treeless gaps. Deep rooted eucalypts are often given as an "example" of the highly water consuming exotics, but a range of other tree species may show similar relative increases in water use, compared to the natural forest in a given site. In South Africa, the water consumption of trees is recognised in water management. To establish a wood lot or plantation requires special permission from local forest and water authorities, and is associated with specific fees and costs as it will decrease water available for other uses in landscape. One reason for increased water consumption in afforested areas is the use of exotic, more water consuming species, compared to the native vegetation.

We conclude that forest water use is often a significant factor in landscape water flows, including surface, sub-surface and downstream. But the specific impact on the water resources of deforestation and afforestation is governed not only by site specific soil and topographic conditions, but also by whether species are native or exotic; whether trees are in large homogenous plantations or in a landscape and stand structure mosaic. The water use and partitioning of a forest stand is also relative to the site's natural or alternative landuses and water balance flows. Due to the complexity of forests and their impacts on the local water balance, few comprehensive case studies exist for each climatic, vegetative and hydrological response, especially for semi-arid tropical regions with previously forested, now degraded, soils. In contrast the few studies available are from southern Africa and India where former non-forested grasslands and savannas have been afforested. Thus, the lack of data and empirical evidence is seriously challenging our ability to assess potential water balance impacts by deforestationor afforestation in specific landscape contexts.

Synergies and trade offs in miombo woodlands, southern Africa

Miombo woodland is a significant biome covering about 10 % of the African landmass (Fig. 5.1), approximately 2.5 – 4 million km² depending on definition (White, 1983; Millington et al., 1994). It supports the livelihood of 100 million people in the area or outside, relying on products from this distinct and unique biome (Campbell *et al.*, 2007). Major provisional ecosystem services essential for livelihoods are charcoal for rural and urban energy, water for downstream needs, wood, meat from grazing and hunting, fruit, tourism, and habitat provision, etc. In addition, the woodland affects several regulatory services, such as landscape water flows, soil erosion control and regeneration of soil health in the smallholder systems. Throughout its physically varied region, miombo woodlands overlap with deciduous forests and open savannahs (Frost *et al.*, 1986). The climate is semi-arid with one wet season, but annual rainfall ranges as much as 550 – 1200 mm and dry season lasts between 3 and 7 months. The miombo woodlands also coincide with some of the poorest sub-Saharan African countries, with relatively low rates of achievement of many Millennium Development Goals relating to water supply and sanitation. The high prevalence of HIV/AIDS among other diseases is a big challenge to the people living in the area.

Deforestation is an old and ongoing process in the miombo region (FAO, 2007), but large areas are still covered by miombo in various states. Long term human impacts are often profound on forest structure and species composition in many areas (Campbell *et al.*, 2007). Forest management and tree planting mostly has been focussed on exotic species in plantations and woodlots, even if, more recently, there are increasing numbers of interesting examples of natural forest management in Zimbabwe (Gerhart and Nemarundwe, 2006) and elsewhere (Campbell *et al.*, 2007). Tanzania and Zimbabwe are the central concerned miombo countries that have the most forest plantations. Total areas are still moderate and about half of them are industrial (Varmola and Del Lungo, 2002). Looking ahead, with increasing demands for energy, industrial wood and carbon credits, there is a growing interest in plantation forestry in the relatively sparsely populated miombo region, not least in Tanzania (e.g., Stave, 2006). The miombo landscape provides a very varied structure and net primary productivity of the continuum ranges from degraded miombo to well-managed miombo to even-aged forest plantations. This has large impact on water management, both through water use by the trees as well as by the impact on soils and potential groundwater recharge (Malmer and Nyberg, 2008). Any major change in the miombo woodlands needs serious consideration: can the 'sponge effect' be lost? And what implications does that have on provisioning and

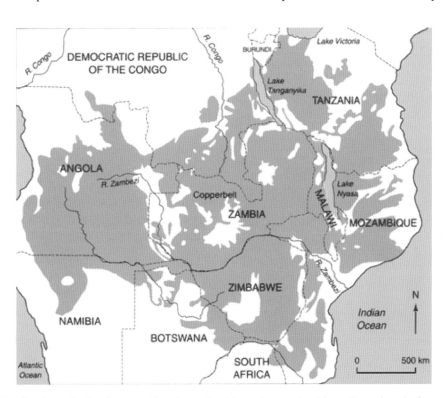

Figure 5.1. Distribution of miombo woodlands, major biome in semi-arid southern hemisphere Africa.

regulating ecosystem services supporting vulnerable livelihoods in the area?

An example of the altered water balance due to the planting of exotic species is the decreased lower annual and dry season stream flows in areas populated by *Eucalyptus saligna* compared to nearby grasslands in Sao Hill, Tanzania; the stream flow reduction by *Pinus patula* was much less (Mhando, 1991). Thus, planting eucalyptus could potentially mean a loss of biodiversity, and reduced dry season flows. In another study, using long term data, Kashaigili *et al.* (2006) show major decreases in dry season flows (60-70%) between 1958 and 2004, downstream of the Usangu wetlands in Tanzania. In the upstream areas, woodlands have decreased strongly due to expansion of cultivated lands and bare land. In this case it may be tempting to hypothesise on the "lost sponge effect", but Kashaigili *et al.* (2006) used modelling to show that the major reason for declining dry season flows was due to increase of irrigated agriculture upstream from the wetlands.

A healthy soil system is key for catching rainfall

Management of organic material in soils is crucial for a healthy soil system. Soil organic matter influences soil physical characteristics and availability of plant nutrients. Increased soil organic matter increases soil water storage capacity, and water infiltration capacity. Harvesting, grazing and fire lead to degradation by reducing litterfall; i.e., contributing to reduced organic

matter content, and oxidation. In miombo, already low topsoil organic contents are typically reduced by up to 50 % by agriculture (Walker and Desanker, 2004). Soil organic matter also determines top soil physical properties. The soil structure (soil aggregates increasing the amount of large pores) determines to a large extent the partitioning between surface runoff, erosion and soil water infiltration (Bruijnzeel, 1990; Malmer *et al.*, 2005). In various land uses in Zambia, the structural stability of the soil was shown to be positively related to soil organic carbon (King and Campbell, 1993). Soil crusting is a common reason for reduced soil water infiltration in semi-arid areas. Perroll and Sandström (1995) concluded that vegetation cover was the other major determinant apart from soil texture in Tanzania and Botswana. Similarly, Casenave and Valentin (1992),using data from 87 sites in semi-arid West Africa, found intensity of surface sealing, vegetative cover and soil faunal activity to be determinants of soil water infiltration. Organic matter in the soil is highly dependant on vegetation species composition. Research suggests that miombo may not always be superior to exotic species, but the condition of the miombo stand does affect the litter, the soil organic matter and subsequently the infiltration of rainfall (Ilstedt *et al.*,2007; Ngegba *et al.*,2001; King and Campbell, 1993; Nord, 2008) (Fig. 5.2).

In the miombo region, like other semi-arid areas, a higher intensity of land use in trees is already leading to environmental degradation. Despite inadequate scientific clarity in regard to the biophysical processes and lack of empirical data, resources have to be managed. Multi-species plantations in general are shown by meta-analysis to be more productive than mono-specific plantations (Piotto, 2008). At the same time these more complex forest stand types might have a more favourable impact on infiltration and a more moderate water demand compared to most even-aged monocultures. In addition, experiences of development of smallholder involvement in forest establishment and management from Asia might be fruitful to apply in the miombo region (Nawir *et al.*, 2007).

West African parklands – trees in agriculture generate soil and water gains

Sudano-Sahelian parklands stem from dry deciduous forests with some relation to miombo. These parklands have had strong human influence on the structure of the vegetation for a long time. While small-scale shifting

Typical miombo woodland   Malmer

cultivation is dominant in miombo (Campbell *et al.*, 1996), the parkland of West Africa is dominantly under permanent traditional agroforestry with dense wooded savannah. There is an abundance of preferred indigenous tree species (Pullan, 1974). The fallow periods are continuously being shortened because of pressure for land (Boffa, 2000). However, farmers retain trees in farmlands for their own livelihood purposes.

Certain species such as *Vitellaria* provide valuable butter from the kernels of the tree nuts. This is used for local consumption and provides an important source of income for rural women (Kelly *et al.*, 2004). Products from several tree species are also used in traditional medicine and produce edible fruits. However, due to the intensification of agriculture (mainly the use of tractors) in the region, the parklands are decreasing and in many cases the tree cover is diminishing (Nikiéma, 2005). Several studies have shown that trees add soil organic matter through litter fall as well as promoting biological activity in the soil (Young, 1995) and thereby improve the physical properties of the soil (e.g., Traoré *et al.*, 2004). These benefits are similar to the effects of applying compost manure to the fields (Ouédraogo *et al.*, 2001).

Little is known from research about the effects of trees on the water management of the parklands, although vegetative cover in the region is considered to be important to ensure maximum rainwater infiltration into the soil profile (Casenave and Valentin, 1992; Hansson, 2006). In addition, Bayala *et al.* (2003) concluded from a study carried out in the parklands of Burkina Faso that an application of leaf litter mulch from *Parkia biglobosa* and *Vitellaria paradoxa* prunings improved soil organic matter content as well as water infiltration. More recent Bayala *et al.* (2008) have shown some parkland trees to hydraulically redistribute water during the dry season. This means that the trees at night transport water from deeper soil layers to the top soil. This is beneficial for both the trees and other plants during hot dry season days. However, as for miombo, there has not been clear scientific verification of the effect of the trees on water budgets. The effect on rainfall by re-introducing trees and their management in the parklands also has not been clearly synthesized and interpreted.

On a field scale, *in situ* rainwater harvesting can enhance re-establishment of trees on the landscape. The success of re-greening of the Central Plateau, Burkina Faso (Reij and Smaling, 2008) is an example where land reclamation through *in situ* water harvesting has led to increased numbers of trees on former crop-land (Reij *et al.*, 2003). In this case, the severe droughts generated a positive response in terms of activating communities and mobilizing resources to address multiple challenges including poverty, low crop yields and severe land degradation. Farmers, NGOs, local government and

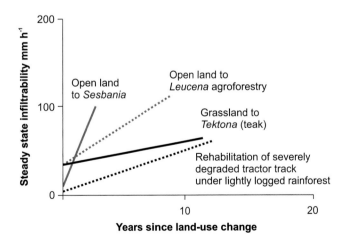

Figure 5.2: Examples of efficiency of rehabilitation of water infiltration capacity after planting trees of different species and in different situations: open land to Sesbania, open land to Leucena agroforestry, grassland to Tektona (teak) and rehabilitation of severely degraded tractor track under lightly logged rainforest (after Ilstedt et al., 2007)

external funders together enabled the adoption of *in situ* rainwater harvesting for growing crops and trees. A few key technologies were particularly interesting such as the *zai* pitting, and the construction of stone bunds and gully control structures. The results of *in situ* rainwater harvesting showed that average crop yields doubled over 20 years, producing more forage leading to increased livestock numbers and establishment of more trees (citing Riej *et al.*, 2003). In addition, species diversity in fauna was regenerated, and a noticeable rise occurred in the groundwater table. Although soil fertility has improved through better soil and water management, there is more potential for improvement. According to the local communities, food security has improved to meet the demand of the population, that has increased by 25% between 1984 and 1996. An important effect of improved yields is that no further crop land expansion has occurred since mid 1980s despite the population growth and improved livelihoods.

Productive parkland in Sahel　　　Malmer

Trees removed in lack of knowledge for total valuation?

Removal of trees and lack of regeneration in the parkland is often driven by the introduction of mechanized farming in a cotton and maize rotation system. This is for increased food production and cash incomes for local communities. However in the long term, this production system may lead to a decline in soil organic matter, fertility, high erosion risk and soil degradation (Lal, 1993). Maintaining soil organic matter is important

for carbon sequestration and better moisture retention for improved crop harvest (Ouattara, 2007). This is instrumental for climate change adaptation where scenarios indicate drier climates in years to come.

In contrast to increasing demands for higher biomass production and increased crop yields, and in view of the lack of reliable data on trees and their benefits, it is not easy to motivate people on economic and long term benefits of trees in parklands. There is a lack of clear validation systems for evaluating the effect of retaining trees in parklands. Carbon trading systems have not been fully successful in providing this validation, but it is expected that the recognition of such systems in the post-Kyoto protocols for REDD (Reducing Emissions from Deforestation and Degradation) might be one way.

5.4 CONCLUSIONS

We conclude that cases of forestry and of a landscape mosaic with trees can be seen as 'rainwater harvesting interventions', where the forests and trees provides numerous provisional, regulatory, aesthetic and supporting ecosystem services for sustaining livelihoods and producing economic benefit. The notion of forests being 'water towers' is a misconception, as forests and trees actually consume water in generating the ecosystem services. However, this 'lost' water creates other benefits in terms of human welfare via the goods and services provided by the forest ecosystems. Depending on local conditions, forest areas can act as sponges, ensuring stable base-flows in downstream river systems, as well as increasing water infiltration into the soil, which can recharge shallow groundwater sources.

Degraded parklands in Sahel　　　Malmer

However, the cases of water partitioning in semi-arid miombo woodlands and West African parklands cannot be generalized to locations with different species and management strategies. The lack of empirical evidence of linkages between trees, landscapes and rainfall complicates the issue of possible tradeoffs or mutual benefits to be derived from trees, or in terms of ecosystem services and landscape water flows (green and blue water partitioning of rainfall). As Scott *et al.* (2005) express, possibly in most cases, productive forests might use more water than they contribute to groundwater recharge. On the other hand, with increasing demands for high levels of production of both wood and food, the alternative, with continued deforestation and continued deterioration of forests, parklands and their soils, is hardly a viable alternative.

The 'rainwater harvesting' effect of trees and forests is turned into valuable goods and services and is also linked to the impact on the soil surface and the actual consumption of water. Trees generate litter, which improves the organic matter content in soils - a key component to increased water infiltration. Secondly, trees reduce rainfall impacts on soil surfaces that control soil erosion and sediment transport. Although there is limited empirical data on water balances and forests, the well-known benefits of forest ecosystem services can offer a positive regeneration of degraded and water stressed landscapes. Improved provisioning of goods and services as wood, fodder, fruit, medicines, sometimes water flows as well as habitats for diverse flora and fauna are all components that are enhancing the livelihoods of smallholder farmers. Additional benefits such as water purification, build-up of fertile soil systems, and reduced flooding and sediment transport are all complementary benefits for a local community. However, extensive land-use changes from forests to plantations or to decreased forest cover should always be weighed within a comprehensive impact assessment of both environmental and social-economic issues, including the landscape water balance.

Sahelina parkland Mali   Enfors

REFERENCES

Bayala, J., Mando, A., Ouedraogo, S.J. and Teklehaimanot, Z., 2003. Managing Parkia biglobosa and Vitellaria paradoxa Prunings for Crop Production and Improved Soil Properties in the Sub-Sudanian Zone of Burkina Faso. Arid Land Res & Man, 17(3): 283 - 296.

Bayala, J., Heng, L.K., van Noordwijk, M. and Ouedraogo, S.J., in press. Hydraulic redistribution study in two native tree species of agroforestry parklands of West African dry savanna. Acta Oecologica, (2008) Boffa, J.M., 2000. Les parcs agroforestiers en Afrique subsaharienne. Cahier FAO Conservation, 34.

Bruijnzeel, L.A. 1989. (De)forestation and dry season flow in the tropics: a closer look. J Trop For Sci, 1: 145–161.

Bruijnzeel, L. A. 1990. Hydrology of moist tropical forests and effects of conversion: A state of knowledge review. UNESCO – IHP, Humid Tropics Programme, Paris.

Bruijnzeel, L.A. 2004. Hydrological functions of tropical forests: not seeing the soil for the trees? Agric, Ecos & Env 104: 185-228.

Campbell, B., Frost, P.G.H. and Byron, N., 1996. Miombo woodlands and their use: Over view and key issues. In: The Miombo in Transition: Woodlands and Wellfare in Africa, B. Campbell (ed.). CIFOR, Bogor, Indonesia, pp 1-10.

Campbell, B.M., Angelsen, A., Cunningham, A., Katerere, Y., Sitoe, A. And Wunder, S. 2007. Miombo woodlands – opportunities and barriers to sustainable forest management. CIFOR, Bogor, Indonesia http://www.cifor.cgiar.org/miombo/docs/Campbell_BarriersandOpportunities.pdf (4th November 2008)

Casenave, A.and Valentin, C. 1992. A runoff capability classification system based on surface features criteria in semi-arid areas of West Africa. J Hydrol, 130: 231-249.

FAO 2007. State of the World's Forests 2007. Food and Agriculture Organization of theUnited Nations, Rome, Italy. 140p.

Farley, K.A., Jobbágy, G. and Jackson, R.B. 2005. Effects of afforestation on water yield: a global synthesis with implications for policy. Glob Ch Biol, 11, 1565–1576.

Frost, P.G.H., Medina, E., Menaut, J.C., Solbrig, O., Swift, M. and Walker, B., 1986. Responses of savannas to stress and disturbance. Biol. Int. 10: 1-78.

Hansson, L., 2006. Comparisons of Infiltrability Capacities in Different Parklands and Farming Systems of Semi-Arid Burkina Faso. MSc Thesis, Swedish University of Agricultural Science, Umeå, 20 pp.

Hurni H, Tato K., (eds) 1992. Erosion, conservation and small-scale farming. International Soil Conservation Organisation and World Association of Soil and Water Conservation, Bern.

Ilstedt, U., Malmer, A., Verbeeten, E. and Murdiyarso, D. 2007. The effect of afforestation on water infiltration in the tropics: a systematic review and meta-analysis. For Ecol & Man, 251, 45–51.

Kaimowitz, D. 2005. Useful myths and intractable truths: the politics of the link between forests and water in Central America. In: Forest-water-people in the humid tropics (eds Bonell M, Bruijnzeel LA), pp. 86–98. Cambridge University Press, Cambridge.

Kashaigili, J.J., McCartney, M.P., Mahoo, H.F., Lankford, B.A., Mbilinyi, B.P., Yawson, D.K. and Tumbo, S.D. 2006. Use of a Hydrological Model for Environmental Management of the Usangu Wetlands, Tanzania. IWMI Research Report, 104. http://www.iwmi.cgiar.org/Publications/IWMI_Research_Reports/index.aspx (7 November 2008).

Kelly, B.A., Bouvet, J.M. and Picard, N., 2004. Size class distribution and spatial pattern of Vitellaria paradoxa in relation to farmers' practices in Mali. Agrofor Sys, 60(1): 3-11.

King, J.A. and Campbell, B.M. 1993. Soil organic matter relations in five land cover types in the miombo region (Zimbabwe). For Ecol & Man, 67: 225-239.

Lal, R., 1993. Tillage effect on soil degradation, soil resilience, soil quality and sustainability. Soil Till. Res, 27: 1-8.

Malmer, A., van Noordwijk, M. and Bruijnzeel, L.A. 2005. Effects of shifting cultivation and forest fire. In: Bonell, M., Bruijnzeel, L.A. (Eds.), Forest-water-people in the humid tropics: Past present and future hydrological research for integrated land and water management. Cambridge University Press, Cambridge, pp. 533-560.

Malmer, A. and Nyberg, G., 2008. Forest and water relations in miombo woodlands: need for understanding of complex stand management. In: Varmola, M., Valkonen, S. and Taipanen, S. (eds), Research and development for sustainable management of semiarid/miombo/woodlands in East Africa. Working Papers of the Finnish Forest Research Institute 98: 70-86. http://www.metla.fi/julkaisut/workingpapers/2008/mwp098.htm (in press)

Mhando, L.M. 1991. Forest hydrological studies in Eucalyptus saligna, Pinus patula and grassland catchments at Sao Hill, Tanzania. MSc thesis, Stencils series, 17, Department of Forest Site Research, Swedish University of Agricultural Science, Umeå, Sweden.

Millington, A. C., Chritchley, R. W., Douglas, T. D. and Ryan, P. 1994. Prioritization of indigenous fruit tree species based on formers evaluation criteria: some preliminary results from central region, Malawi. In: Proceedings of the regional conference on indigenous fruit trees of the Miombo ecozone of Southern Africa, Mangochi, Malawi, January 23–27 1994, 97–105. ICRAF, Nairobi.

Nikiéma, A., 2005. Agroforestry Parkland Species Diversity:Uses and Management in Semi-Arid West Africa (Burkina Faso). PhD thesis, Wageningen University, Wageningen.

Nord, H. 2008. Water infiltration under different land use in miombo woodlands outside Morogoro, Tanzania. MSc thesis, Department of Forest Ecology and Management, Swedish University of Agriculture, Sweden, 2008: 34.

Ouédraogo, E., Mando, A. and Zombré, N.P., 2001. Use of compost to improve soil properties and crop productivity under low input agricultural system in West Africa. Agric, Ecos & Env.84(3): 259-266.

Ouattara, K., 2007. Improved soil and water conservatory managements for cotton-maize rotation system in the western cotton area of Burkina Faso. PhD Thesis, Swedish University of Agricultural Science, Umeå.

Piotto, D. 2008. A meta-analysis comparing tree growth in monocultures and mixed plantations. Forest Ecol. Man. 255: 781-786.

Pullan, R.A. 1974. Farmed parklands in West Africa. Savanna, 3: 119-151.

Reij, C., G.Tappan, A. Belvemire. 2005. Changing land management practises and vegetation on the Central Plateau of Burkina Faso (1968-2002). J.Arid Env. 63:642-659

Reij, C.P.; Smaling, E.M.A. 2008. Analyzing successes in agriculture and land management in Sub-Saharan Africa: Is macro-level gloom obscuring positive micro-level change? Land Use Policy 25 (3). - p. 410 - 420.

Sandström, K. 1998. Can forests 'provide' water: widespread myth or scientific reality? Ambio, 27, 132–138.

Scott, D.F., Bruijnzeel, L.A. and Mackensen, J. 2005. The hydrological and soil impacts of forestation in the tropics. In: Forest-water-people in the humid tropics (eds Bonell M, Bruijnzeel LA), pp. 622–651. Cambridge University Press, Cambridge.

Stave, J. 2000. Carbon Upsets: Norwegian "Carbon Plantations" in Tanzania. In: Negative Impact of Large-scale Monoculture Tree Plantations, Friends of the Earth International in cooperation with the World Rainforest Movement and FERN, http://www.wrm.org.uy/actors/CCC/trouble6.html (4th November 2008)

Traoré, K., Ganry, F., Oliver, R. and Gigou, J., 2004. Litter Production and Soil Fertility in a Vitellaria paradoxa Parkland in a Catena in Southern Mali. Arid Land Res Man, 18(4): 359-368.

Varmola, M. and Del Lungo (editors), 2002. Forest plantation areas 1995 data set. Forestry Department, Food and Agriculture Organization of the United Nations, Rome, Forest Plantations Working Papers, FP/18. http://www.fao.org/DOCREP/005/Y7204E/y7204e00.htm#Contents (4th November 2008)

Walker, S.M. and Desanker, P.W. 2004. The impact of land use on soil carbon in Miombo Woodlands of Malawi. Fort Ecol Man, 203: 345-360.

White, F. 1983. The vegetation of Africa. Natural resources Research 20, UNESCO, Paris.

Young, A., 1995. L'agroforestrie pour la conservation du sol. CTA, Wageningen, Pays Bas. 194 p.

CHAPTER 6

RAINWATER HARVESTING FOR WATER SECURITY IN RURAL AND URBAN AREAS

Main author: Klaus W. König, Überlingen, Germany

Contributing authors:
Johann Gnadlinger, Brazilian Rainwater Catchment and Management Association, (ABCMAC), Juazeiro, Brazil
Mooyoung Han, Seoul National University, Seoul, Republic of Korea
Hans Hartung, FAKT-Consult, Weikersheim, Germany
Günter Hauber-Davidson, Water Conservation Group Pty Ltd., Sydney, Australia
Andrew Lo, Chinese Culture University, Taipei, Taiwan
Zhu Qiang, Gansu Research Institute for Water Conservancy, Wuxi City, China

6.1   INTRODUCTION

At the 2000 UN Millennium Summit, world leaders from rich and poor countries alike committed themselves to eight time-bound goals as a blue print to accelerate development. The resultant plan is set forth in the Millennium Development Goals (MDGs). Goal 7 addressed the environment and water. Its targets include the goal to *"halve, by 2015, the proportion of the population without sustainable access to safe drinking water and basic sanitation"*. In relation to water, this implies provision of safe water for drinking as well as for hygiene. And because these amounts are relatively small (compared with e.g., agriculture) there are large

Fetching water from a dry river bed in Mozambique
Chang/UNEP

potentials to exploit rainwater harvesting in this context of human well-being.

Halfway through to the 2015 targets, globally, the target related to drinking water is expected to be met, but not the sanitation target. Nevertheless, these global figures mask a critical situation in some regions. For example, sub-Saharan Africa and Oceania will not meet these targets at the present rate of implementation. With 2.4 billion persons without access to sanitation in 2004, the target will also be missed, particularly in South Asia, East Asia and sub-Saharan Africa. To meet the target requires doubling the efforts of the last 15 years for

Development domains for rooftop Rainwater Harvesting in Africa   UNEP/Khaka

Water carrying in Bhutan, India　　　　UNEP/Khaka

sanitation, and increasing those made for drinking water by a third.

Though only one target addresses water, it plays a critical role in meeting the goals, particularly those concerning hunger, poverty, health and biodiversity. To meet the MDGs often assumes a reliable source of good quality water. As an example, the MDG water target focuses on infrastructure, policies, awareness creation, etc. with little attention to the sustainable management of the water sources. Available freshwater continues to decline due to over-abstraction, pollution and reduced precipitation, resulting in a decrease in runoff. An estimated 1.8 billion will live in water scarce areas and two- thirds in water stressed areas by 2050. Climate change will worsen the situation. Ecosystems play an important part in water availability and vice versa, but the link between ecosystems and water availability is complex and not fully understood.

Freshwater ecosystems link directly and indirectly with human well-being, especially the well-being of poor communities and households. There is a close interdependency between freshwater ecosystems and human well-being. Though it is not easy to put

an economic value on ecosystem services, some attempts have been made. The Millennium Ecosystem Assessment found that 60% of the ecosystems assessed were in global decline, particularly the aquatic ones, with detrimental effects to human well-being. A significant cause of ecosystem degradation is over-abstraction for water supply. Rainwater harvesting can be used to improve ecosystem function, particularly the water supply aspect, and regulation (controlling flood and erosion). Globally, there is a significant untapped potential in rainwater which can be harvested to improve ecosystem services and human well-being. This chapter addresses the contribution of rainwater in improving ecosystem services related to rural and urban water supplies.

6.2 RAINWATER HARVESTING, ECOSYSTEMS AND RURAL WATER SUPPLY

Most people living in rural areas depend on development which is based on ecosystem services. Typical rural ecosystem services that support human livelihoods include water supply, agriculture including livestock management, fisheries, and forest and tree products (timber, honey, fruit, vegetables, fibres, fuel etc.). In many parts of Africa, wild fruit, firewood and charcoal are major sources of income, especially in times of crop failure. Ecosystems are also necessary for water purification, erosion regulation, waste treatment and disease regulation. Support services include soil formation (providing good soils for agriculture and vegetation). Degradation of these ecosystem services is threatening the achievement of the MDGs.

About one sixth of the world population – a total of 1.1 billion people – remains without access to improved drinking water, and 84% of these live in rural areas. In addition, 2 of the 2.6 billion people without access to basic sanitation live in rural areas (UNICEF& WHO, 2006). The figure differs according to regions. For example, in 2004, in sub-Saharan African rural areas, the number of people who were not provided with improved drinking water was five times higher and those without access to sanitation were three times higher than those living in urban areas. Poverty is also much higher in the rural areas.

In rural communities, water is required for drinking and agricultural purposes. Rainwater harvesting is highly decentralized and enables individuals and communities to manage their own water for these purposes. This is particularly suitable in rural areas with a dispersed population and where a reticulated water supply is not feasible or extremely costly for investment. The low cost of the rainwater harvesting technologies can be a more attractive investment option in rural areas.

In addition to water for drinking and sanitation, fishing, animal husbandry and agriculture are the major activities in rural areas which all depend on a reliable water supply to be productive. As shown in Chapters 3 and 4, rainwater harvesting can also help meet the demands for water for these purposes. There are numerous cases where rainwater harvesting is used to improve livelihoods by providing water for domestic purposes; for subsistence and income generation activities such as gardening, and livestock rearing; for environmental purposes, through recharging groundwater and establishing woodlots to reduce deforestation. In essence, it can supply water to accelerate social and economic development, to alleviate poverty and generate income for rural farmers by enhancing the crop yield, modifying the method of production, as well as to promoting environmental conservation.

Agro-pastoralists enhance livelihoods through better water supply in Kenya

In Kaijado and Lare, in the semi-arid savannah of Kenya, rainwater harvesting provides water for drinking, sanitation, and enhancing the productivity of the agro-eco systems (Appendix II: Case 6.1). The technologies introduced consisted of roof-water harvesting for domestic purposes (drinking and sanitation), runoff collection in ponds for small gardens, trenches for groundwater recharge and afforestation. For sustainability, the project included a micro-finance component, where the community was trained to manage credits before borrowing money from commercial institutions.

The project has enhanced the ecosystem functioning by recharging groundwater, increasing the volume of water stored, and reducing soil erosion through the family woodlots that reduced runoff-related erosion. Once the planted trees have matured, the women will use them for fuel, contributing to the reduction of deforestation, which is a major problem in the area.

Family livelihoods improved from selling vegetables and income generation activities such bee-keeping and

Working together to dig a run off RWH pond

UNEP/Khaka

Harambee constructing water storage in Kenya

Hartung

crafts. The community can now borrow money from commercial micro-finance companies which they use for productive activities. Since the establishment of the micro-finance component, all of the members have been paid on time, and there have not been any arrears. Providing water to schools enabled girls to attend during their period of menstruation, thereby increasing their attendance.

Adapting water supply in semi-arid Brazil through rainwater harvesting

The semi-arid region of Brazil (SAB), in the northeastern part of the country, has a rainfall which can range from below 185 mm to 974 mm between one year and the next. It is concentrated within a few weeks of the year and is associated with a high evaporation rate of 3,000 mm a year. In 2005, the Ministry of National Integration calculated its drought risk between 1970 and 1990 as being above 60%. Climate change forecasts indicate that the drier parts of the SAB will become even drier, despite there being a small increase in precipitation. To adapt to the current rainfall variability, more water storage is needed in rural areas. Rainwater harvesting is one way to adapt to current and future rainfall variability. The Program for 1 Million Cisterns (P1MC) (Appendix II case 6.3) was initiated to supply safe drinking water for 1 million rural households (five million people). With funding from the government and the private sector, more than 230,000 cisterns were constructed as of August 2008 with some municipalities constructing their own.

Evaluation of the program found that the health of the population improved through better drinking water quality and time saved for women, who no longer need to fetch water over long distances to their homes

(Ministry of Environment, 2006; Silva, 2006). From an ecosystem service perspective, rainwater harvesting and storage has impacted farm productivity in numerous ways. Using water for the irrigation of higher value crops, such as in kitchen gardens, especially off-season has been beneficial for household food supplies and incomes. Rainwater harvesting has also resulted in an increased number of goats per household, partly as more fodder is available. On the land, observed changes include: reduced erosion through the practice of conservation tillage and construction of soil bunds, reduced flooding downstream, and increased species diversity due to infiltration banks and sub-surface storage dams. So far, the effects of rainwater harvesting have not affected water supplies downstream.

Rainwater harvesting has been accepted by the rural community in the SAB (Gnadlinger, 2006) who have learned to live in harmony with nature in a semi-arid climate, and are ready to fight for it, as well as for all the other aspects which might improve their livelihoods. They understand that water must be managed in an integrated way, taking into consideration the source (rain, surface water, soil and ground water), and water uses (for environment, domestic, agricultural and emergency purposes).

Small rainwater storage improves livelihood for 15 million people in China

Gansu Province is one of the driest, most mountainous and poorest regions in China. It has an annual precipitation of 330 mm while potential evaporation is as high as 1,500-2,000 mm. Rain is the only water available and reticulated water systems are not feasible because of the terrain and the sparse population. This is an area lacking in three essentials: water, food and fuel. This causes insecurity in both human livelihoods and the environment. From 1988 to 1992, research was conducted to find the most suitable rainwater harvesting interventions to promote in the area. By the end of 1994, 22,800 updated water cellars with 2.4 million m^2 of new catchment area (tiled roof and concrete lined courtyard) had been built. A total of 28,000 families (141,000 people), 43,000 large livestock and 139,000 small animals got enough water to drink.

Rainwater harvesting also played a significant role in promoting ecological and environmental conservation. The "Land Conversion" Program for the north and northwest China, along with development of rainwater

Tank no 84,625 in P1MC   Gnadlinger

harvesting, increased the area of orchards. In the period 1996 to 2000, 73,300 ha of land were irrigated with water supplied through the rainwater harvesting, with the irrigated areas used for the planting of trees in Longnan Prefecture. In Yongjing County, 273 ha of trees were planted, using the rainwater harvesting system. The productivity of farm land has increased, with the introduction of the rain water harvesting systems. Yields have improved by 20-40% in the fields, kitchen gardens and holdings of pigs and sheep. Species diversity has increased, since rainwater harvesting enables greater diversity of crops and cropping patterns. As incomes rise, people no longer need to degrade their landscape to support livelihoods. One key improvement in the environment introduced through rainwater harvesting is reduced soil erosion, which maintains better soil quality on site, and reduces siltation in waterways and dams downstream. Reduced incidences of flooding downstream indicate another positive effect of the rainwater harvesting interventions upstream.

The rainwater harvesting approach that has been adopted since the late 1980s has brought about tremendous changes in the rural parts of the dry, mountainous areas of China. Experiences with rainwater harvesting during the past 20 years show that rainwater harvesting is a strategic and invaluable measure for achieving integrated development in the rural areas. Statistics show that, by adopting rainwater harvesting techniques, 15 million people have solved their drinking water problems and 2.6 million ha of land have been irrigated. Other intermediate techniques such as rudimentary greenhouses, solar heating, and the indigenously innovated underground tanks have also been adopted.

Use of rainwater harvesting systems for domestic water supply, agriculture and drought mitigation has spread to the semi-humid and humid areas of China that suffer from drought, such as Southwest China, the coastal towns of Southeast China, the islands and Guangxi Autonomous Region.

6.3 RAINWATER HARVESTING IMPROVES URBAN WATER SECURITY AND REDUCES COSTS

The world's urban population increased from about 200 million (15% of world population) in 1900 to 2.9 billion (50% of world population) in 2000, and the number of cities with populations in excess of 1 million increased from 17 in 1900 to 388 in 2000 (McGranahan *et al.*, 2005). As people increasingly live in cities, and as cities act as both human ecosystem habitats and drivers of ecosystem change, it will become increasingly important to foster urban systems that contribute to human well-being and reduce ecosystem service burdens at every level. Severe environmental health problems occur within urban settlements, resulting from inadequate access to ecosystem services, such as clean water. Many ecosystems in and around urban areas are more bio-diverse than are rural monocultures, and they can also provide food, water services, comfort, social amenities, cultural values, and so on, particularly if they are well managed. Moreover, urban areas currently only account for about 2.8% of the total land area of Earth, despite containing about half the world's population.

Impacts of urban hydrology on ecosystems
Cities require large amounts of water to sustain themselves, owing to the sheer size of population and density of housing. Up to now the most typical method of meeting this demand has been to build a large dam or withdraw water from groundwater sources and pipe it in as needed. This can be ecologically disruptive, as well as costly, causing water stress in the river downstream, and changing the biodiversity of the region. In addition, groundwater levels may decline in urban areas as a result of increased pumping as well as extensive areas of impermeable surfaces, with hardly any natural infiltration. In urban areas rainwater is disposed of most commonly as storm flows, in underground pipes, and as quickly as possible. Concentrated storm flows can alter surface water flow patterns, affect flora and fauna, and potentially increase the risk of flood damage downstream. The lack of surface water in urban environments can

Women fetchng water from pond   UNEP/Khaka

cause the dry micro-climate to increase in cities, the so called 'heat island' effect. This leads to a greater need for cooling systems (requiring more electrical power, which increases CO_2 emissions, etc.).

If climate change brings higher peaks and intensities in the volume of precipitation, current stormwater drainages will be too small to cope and more incidences of flooding may occur. The problem of financing the water supply and wastewater infrastructure will increase as a result of demographic changes and urban-rural settlement shifts. However, we have to adapt our technologies of urban hydrology to this change in demography and climate. This is our chance to modernize these very important infrastructure elements for the benefit of the economy and society, by making them decentralised, and thus more affordable (Hiessl, 2008). Cities have access to rainfall, which can be used to supplement water abstractions from surface or groundwater sources and help meet demand.

Water quality and health

Surface water is often contaminated through the release of industrial and domestic effluents directly into lakes and rivers, and from pesticide and agro-chemical run-off from fields. In theory, rainwater is the safest of all water sources. Although rainwater can become contaminated through the absorption of atmospheric pollutants, it is usually clean as it hits the earth, unless there is atmospheric pollution from industry. The challenge with rainwater is to keep the collection surfaces (roof tops) and the storage facilities free from contamination and free from mosquito breeding. With the adequate operation and maintenance of the collection areas, filter and tank systems, good quality water may be obtained by collecting rainwater from rooftops. While high-quality source water may require little or no treatment, it is still recommended that any water used for drinking be disinfected to ensure microbiological safety. According to the Water, Sanitation and Hygiene programme of WHO, maximum health benefits are achieved if water interventions are accompanied by sanitation and hygiene promotion.

A two-sided coin, synergy advantages

Urbanisation puts the surrounding water resources under pressure, challenging ecosystem services in two principal ways. Firstly, the concentrated urban population demands adequate water for consumption and sanitation needs, which requires stable and large supplies of water, often through the use of surface water/dams or groundwater. These extractions can threaten other landscape habitats and functions, reducing the ecosystem's capacity to supply things such as water downstream, habitat for biodiversity, and livelihood support. Secondly, the reduced infiltration of urban landscapes alters the flow downstream, and can increase the incidence of flooding. Rainwater harvesting in urban areas can address both these negative effects. Rainwater harvesting tanks contribute to the re-distribution of flows over longer temporal scales, thus reducing the incidence of flooding downstream. The additional effect, is that the collected rainwater is used, which means that demand on other water sources can be reduced. Many synergies between water storage and additional non-accounted positive effects have been found for rainwater harvesting projects in urban areas:

- evapotranspiration from planted roofs, retention swales and ponds, cooling down the urban heat island effect in cities, thus improving human well-

Rainwater Harvesting for domestic use on Mallorca Island, Spain   König

being and saving energy for cooling in hot weather periods (reducing the CO_2 footprint, mitigating climate change)

• energy savings due to reduced pumping

• aesthetic values of architectural and landscape water features, created by providing rainwater retention on site

• biodiversity values of planted rooftops, retention swales and ponds, provided by rainwater retention on site, improving ecosystems even in urban areas

• infiltration from retention swales and ponds, recharging groundwater aquifers

• daylight reflection from retention ponds designed close to buildings, lighting up building interiors, thus helping to save energy (reducing the CO_2 footprint, mitigating climate change)

• greater awareness of the ecosystem, when citizens run their own rainwater harvesting system, thus saving not only water, but also other natural resources, e.g. energy. Also usable for education in schools and universities (reducing the CO_2 footprint, mitigating climate change)

• higher concentration of sewage water in mixed sewers, improving the functioning of centralized sewage treatment plants resulting in cleaner outflows to rivers (reducing the impact on ecosystems) and less pumping energy expenditure in the plants, thus reducing costs for the community (enhancing human well-being in socio-financial terms) and mitigating climate change (reducing the CO_2 footprint).

The cases below provide more details and ideas, developed in different regions of the globe.

Revival of rainwater tanks in Australia

Australia is a country that can look back on a long tradition of rainwater utilisation. In recent years, Australia has been facing a water crisis. Increasing population, cheap water, and a failure to add new supplies, exacerbated by the effects of climate change, have brought home a stark reality: some cities have been running out of water. The severe water restrictions placing harsh limitations on the watering gardens and washing of cars along with a strong personal sense of wanting to do something about the water crisis have led to a huge revival in domestic rainwater tanks. Spurred on by generous rebate schemes, Australians just love them. Rainwater tanks have become the latest "must have" item (Appendix II: Case 6.10). This has now spilled over into commercial rainwater harvesting. For new buildings, thanks to the Green Star rating scheme, it is almost a pre-requisite to install a rainwater harvesting system.

Approximately 30% of Australia's urban water consumption is non-residential. A quarter of that could be reduced through water efficiency measures. Of this demand, some 8% could readily be supplied by commercially viable rainwater harvesting schemes. Such projects can capture rainwater from 1,000 to 10,000 m² and more. If schemes collecting storm water (i.e. rainwater including ground surface runoff) were included, collection areas of 50,000 m² and beyond could be achieved. Large rainwater harvesting schemes are of interest to hospitals, works depots, shopping centres, tertiary institutions, military bases, prisons, sports facilities and parks and gardens. The goal is to build an integrated water supply network where the large dam supply systems work hand in hand with thousands of mini-dam supplies, in the form of both residential and commercial rainwater tanks installed throughout the municipal area. In Australia, it would also match the area where the greatest water demands occur with the regions enjoying the greatest rainfalls.

Decentralised water supply at Star City, Seoul

The complete dependence of city water supply and drainage on a centralized system in the age of steady climate change and increasing urbanization is precarious. There are also the issues of an ageing infrastructure and increasing energy costs. These natural and man-made risks can be reduced through the addition of a decentralized water management system.

Star City is a major real estate development project of more than 1,300 apartment units in Gwangjin-gu in the eastern section of Seoul (Appendix II: Case 6.5). The basic design idea of the Rainwater Research Center (RRC) at Seoul National University and Professor Mooyoung Han was to collect up to the first 100 mm of rainwater falling on the complex and to use it for gardening and flushing public toilets. The entire fourth floor below the ground in Building B at Star City is used as a water storage area. Altogether it can store 3,000 m^3 of water, in three separate tanks, with a total floor area of 1,500 m^2. The capacity of each tank is 1,000 m^3.

The first two tanks are used to collect rainwater from the rooftop and the ground that mitigates the danger of a flood in the area during the monsoon season. Collected rainwater is used for the purpose of water conservation. A special feature is that most of the irrigated water in the garden is infiltrated into the ground and returns to the tank for multiple uses. The third tank is used to store tap water in the case of emergency. Fresh tap water is maintained by decanting half of the old water to the rainwater tank and refilling it on a regular basis. Based on the half year operation of the system, water conservation is expected to be approximately 40,000 m^3 per year, which is about 67% of the annual amount of rainfall over the Star City complex. The risk of floods can be controlled pro-actively with the remote control system, by emptying or filling the tanks appropriately. The third novel concept applied in this project was the city government's incentive program for the developer.

Commercial Rainwater Harvesting Woolworths RDC, Minchinbury, Sydney, Australia

Hauber-Davidson

Detached houses, Macquiery Bay, Australia

König

At a broader level, because the decentralized system harvests rainwater on site before it becomes dirty, it reduces the energy required—and therefore the carbon dioxide production and the long-term social cost—for water treatment and transportation. A cost comparison exercise on conventional and rainwater harvesting systems in Seoul City indicated that the energy required to treat and deliver a cubic metre of tap water is 0.2405 kWh, with most of this being energy for transmission. For grey water, treated on site, this would be 1.1177 kWh per cubic metre. According to Prof. Han`s calculations, the same volume of rainwater, needing no treatment, can be delivered for a mere 0.0012 kWh, which is the pumping energy needed to raise the water from storage. The universal imperative is to provide water services with the lowest possible use of energy. Upon evaluation of the Star City project, the city

Rainwater Harvesting tank at hospital, Australia

Hauber-Davidson

government has already passed a city-wide ordinance to promote more rainwater harvesting system installations in development projects.

Taskforce for environment, Bad Hersfeld, Germany

A broad range of medical and care services and 577 beds make the Bad Hersfeld Clinic the center of medical competence for eastern and central Hessen. With approximately 1,400 employees, it is one of the largest employers in the region. Both municipal and private investors are examining operating costs, especially the costs of energy and water. Rainwater utilization in Germany often leads to a double benefit in terms of saving money; namely, the costs for potable water and fees for rainwater disposal (McCann, 2008).

In 1988, an "environmental task force" was established at the clinic. In the first phase of construction, in 1995, rainwater was already utilized for outdoor watering. In addition, a fountain and a pond were supplied with water from the cistern. Since 2001, 111 toilets have been connected to the rainwater system. The cooling of vacuum pumps used for sterilization is especially

effective. Rainwater, at a maximum temperature of 20°C, is circulated through the cistern in a closed system, where the waste heat is re-used (König, 2008). In 2007, with 384 m³ of additional drinking water required during dry periods, the rainwater yield was then 2,180 m³. To this we add the 4,000 m³ of cooling water saved every year making a total of 6,180 m³ of water conserved (Fig. 6.1). Since January 1, 2003, the clinic has also benefited from an amendment to the articles of the city of Bad Hersfeld. The new rate for rainwater per square meter of paved/sealed surface that runs off into the sewage system is 0.66 euros/m² throughout the entire city. Together with the drinking water charge, the Bad Hersfeld Clinic therefore saves €13,500 per year through the utilization of rainwater. The operating costs, including filter maintenance and electricity for the rainwater pumps, are approximately offset by the elimination of the need to soften the cooling water. The savings in energy as a result of the installed rainwater harvesting systems also reduce CO_2 emissions, and give the hospital a smaller carbon footprint.

Germany is among several industrialized countries pioneering a return of this simple but cost effective technique, while also developing rainwater capture systems in new and more sophisticated ways. By supplementing conventional supply, rainwater harvesting has the potential to reduce big, costly and sometimes environmentally-questionable infrastructure projects (Steiner, 2008).

6.4 CONCLUSIONS FROM CASE STUDIES

Rainwater harvesting can provide additional water management options for rural and urban water supply, in developing and developed countries alike. Increasingly, examples from around the world demonstrate how rainwater harvesting for domestic supply can positively address multiple issues regarding safe and reliable water supply, health, and even food and income security, whilst reducing negative impacts on ecosystems, such as over-abstraction of surface and ground waters, or increased incidences of flooding. In addition, implementation can often prove less costly than many traditional, engineered public water supply infrastructure projects.

Rural water supply will continue to be a challenge in many places, due to limited investments and lack of operation and management capacity. Rainwater harvesting has been shown to be an effective way of

Aerial image of Star City, 4 apartment towers with 1,310 apartments, Seoul, Korea　　　POSCO

Site plan of the 4 towers, in total 6.25 ha in Seoul's City Centre, Korea　　　POSCO

providing multiple benefits in rural areas, including health, income and food and water security benefits. In addition, rainwater harvesting has also shown positive synergies in ecosystem service maintenance and enhancement, as well as being cost-efficient. Supporting policies, community and public participation and cost-sharing of investments are prerequisites in enabling these synergies to develop.

To meet Millennium Development Goal targets for sustainable access to safe drinking water and basic sanitation in rural and urban areas we have to make more use of local water resources. It is feasible to use rainwater harvesting to supply rural households with sufficient water to improve livelihoods and sometimes even increase incomes. With appropriate local incentives, such as in Gansu, China, the rainwater

harvesting system developed rapidly and has played a great role in social and economic development over the past 20 years.

Rainwater harvesting in urban areas does not alter hydrological flows in appreciable quantities, as most of the water is returned as sewerage and/or stormwater flows. However, the storage of water may affect downstream users, as the peak and base flows of the discharge curves downstream may be modified. In some instances this is positive, as it reduces incidences of flooding. In other instances it can bring negative impacts on habitats and biodiversity. A second challenge of rainwater harvesting (and any water use) in urban areas is its deteriorating quality if no counter measures are taken, when disposing the water.

Improved local management of water, especially of rainwater, will close the loop and upgrade ecosystems on the community scale. Synergistic effects are the avoidance of urban flooding in the public sewer system, slowing down of runoff from private and public grounds (the community has to charge itself for rainwater runoff from public areas), stimulating rainwater harvesting (thus using less tap water) and/or infiltrating rainwater into the groundwater and/or improving evapotranspiration through infiltration swales, green roofs and evaporation by retention ponds.

All of the case studies above had active policy support in order to enable the implementation and spread of rainwater harvesting structures. One way to increase the implementation of rainwater harvesting is to subsidise initial investment costs. For developing countries,

Aerial image of Bad Hersfeld Clinic, Germany. Harvesting rain from roof tops.　　　Klinik Bad Hersfeld

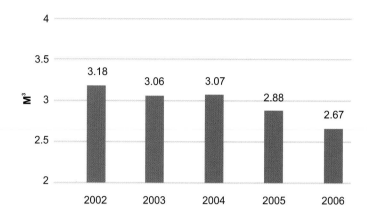

Figure 6.1: Increasing RWH makes decreasing tap water need in Bad Hersfeld Clinic, Germany

Klinik Bad Hersfeld

Rainwater retention pond, aesthetical impact on human wellbeing. Nuremberg Assurance Company, office building, Nuremberg, Germany   König

Vegetables from kajiado   Odour/ICRAF

microfinance credit groups have great advantages. Another is to align legislation regarding water quality, for example, to enable utilisation of rainwater harvesting, with suitable cleaning methods. Sharing knowledge across borders is an effective way to enhance and improve rainwater harvesting in different environments. The focus is always on using appropriate regional technologies for the sustainable operation and maintenance of rainwater harvesting systems by the users and local stakeholders.

REFERENCES

ABCMAC. 2006. Workshop Recommendations about Cistern Water Quality. Petrolina/Brazil, 2006

DIN, 2002. English translation of DIN 1989-1:2001-10 Rainwater harvesting systems. Part 1: Planning, installation, operation and maintenance. Fbr, Darmstadt/Germany

Han M. 2008. Seoul`s Star City: a rainwater harvesting benchmark for Korea. Water 21, p. 17-18. Magazine of the International Water Association, London/UK

Gnadlinger J. 2006. Community water action in semi-arid Brazil, an outline of the factors for success .Official Delegate Publication of the 4th World Water Forum, page 150 – 158, Mexico City/Mexico, March, 16 – 22, 2006

Gnadlinger J. 2008. Rainwater Harvesting Management for Climate Change Adaptation in the Rural Area of Semi Arid Brazil. Presentation at 3rd International Workshop Rainwater Harvesting and Management for Climate Change Adaptation, IWA International Water Association Congress in Vienna/Austria, 11 September 2008

Hauber-Davidson, G. 2008. Große Regenwassersammelanlagen am anderen Ende der Welt. In fbr-wasserspiegel 4/08, p. 18-20. Fachvereinigung für Betriebs- und Regenwassernutzung fbr, Darmstadt/Germany

Hiessl H. 2008. Klimawandel und demografischer Wandel als Herausforderung und Chance. In: König K. W., Ratgeber Regenwasser. Ein Ratgeber für Kommunen und Planungsbüros. Vol. 2, p. 6. Mall, Donaueschingen/Germany

König K. W. 2008. Wirtschaftlichkeit contra Hygiene? Regenwassernutzung im Krankenhaus. In: TAB Technik am Bau,10/2008, p. 78 – 81. Bauverlag, Gütersloh/Germany

McCann, B. 2008. Global prospects of rainwater harvesting. In: Water 21, p. 12-14. Magazine of the International Water Association, London/UK

McGranahan G. et al. 2005. Urban Systems. In: Ecosystems and Human Well-Being, Current State and Trends, Findings of the Condition and Trends Working Group. Millennium Ecosystem Assessment Series Vol. 1, Chapter 27, Island Press, Washington DC/USA

Ministry of the Environment, Secretariat of Water Resources. 2006. National Plan of Water Resources 1st vol., Brasilia

Silva A de S. et al. 2006. Environmental Evaluation of the Performance of the Cisterns Program of MDS and ASA: Executive Summary. EMBRAPA, Brasilia

Steiner A. 2008. Vorwort. In: König K. W., Ratgeber Regenwasser. Ein Ratgeber für Kommunen und Planungsbüros. Vol. 2, p. 3. Mall, Donaueschingen/Germany

UNICEF. 2008. UNICEF Handbook on Water Quality. United Nations Children`s Fund, New York/USA

Zhu Q. 2008. Rainwater harvesting in dry areas. The case of rural Gansu in China, in Tech Monitor, p. 24-30, New Delhi/India, Sep-Oct 2008

Zhu Q. 2003. Rainwater harvesting and poverty alleviation: A case study in Gansu, China, in Water Resources Development, Vol. 19, No. 4

Relevant web-sites for selected case studies in chapter

www.fbr.de/english
www.igb.fraunhofer.de/english
www.skywater.jp
www.rainwater.snu.ac.kr
www.rainwater.org.tw/english
www.abcmac.org.br/english
www.fakt-consult.de

CHAPTER 7

RAINWATER HARVESTING PROVIDING ADAPTATION OPPORTUNITIES TO CLIMATE CHANGE

Main author: Jessica Calfoforo Salas, Kahublagan sang Panimalay Fnd, Iloilo City, Philippines

Contributing authors:
Klaus W. König, Überlingen, Germany
Andrew Lo, Chinese Culture University, Taipei, Taiwan

7.1. INTRODUCTION

The Millennium Ecosystem Assessment (2005) provided a baseline on the state of our ecosystem services. The scenario for the future looks grim given the Millennium Ecosystem Assessment's finding that 60% of the world's ecosystem services have degraded or are being used unsustainably. Many of the degraded ecosystem services were stated to be caused by increased agricultural outputs and expansion. An additional challenge is the 370 million people who were undernourished during the period 1997 to 1999. This figure increased to 852 million during the period 2000 to 2002. These marginalized groups are largely found in South East Asia and the Sub-Saharan Africa.

With the increasing rate of rise in the earth's temperature, the Fourth Assessment Report of the IPCC (2007) projected that by 2020 yields from rainfed agriculture in some countries in Africa could be reduced by up to 50%. With agricultural production and access to food adversely affected, malnutrition and hunger will increase. In Latin America, there is medium confidence in a projection that the number of people at risk of hunger will increase as productivity of important crops and livestock declines, especially in tropical and sub-tropical parts of the continent.

The IPCC Fourth Assessment Report (IPCC, 2007) further states that by mid-century, small islands can be expected to suffer from reduced water supplies to the point where they become insufficient to meet demands, especially during low rainfall periods. In Latin America, changes in precipitation patterns and the disappearance of glaciers are expected to significantly affect fresh water availability thus affecting human consumption, agriculture and energy generation. In Asia, freshwater availability is expected to decrease by 2050 affecting over a billion people. This projection covers Central, South, East and South-East Asia. The onset of water stress comes earlier in Africa. By 2020, between 75 and 250 million people are projected to be affected by increased water stress in this region, in particular in the Mediterranean region in the northern and the southern parts of the continent.

In addition to changing patterns to rainfall amounts, the rainfall events may become more intense (IPCC, 2007). This may affect incidences of flooding and droughts, making the supply of freshwater ecosystem services more unreliable. The Millennium Ecosystem Assessment (2005) examined the regulating services of the ecosystem, and, out of the ten regulating ecosystem services, seven were found to be in decline. In water regulation, according to the report, positive and negative impact varies depending on ecosystem change and location. However, the numbers of flood incidences continue to rise. The centralized water system is the first system to suffer collapse upon the onset of a natural disaster. The GEO4 (2007) reports that one likely impact of climate change will be higher incidence of natural disasters, such as droughts and floods. Two thirds of all natural hazards relate to hydro-meteorological events, such as floods, windstorms and high temperatures. between 1992 and 2001 1.2 billion people were affected by floods.. Ninety per cent of the people exposed to natural hazards reside in the developing countries (GEO4, 2007).

Degradation of ecosystem services in the face of the demands of an increasing population often results in difficult trade-offs, sometimes developing into conflicts. Sometimes, too, it forces people to migrate to even more degraded areas, which further contributes to increasingly unsustainable utilization of natural resources. This perpetuates the vicious cycle of destroying ecosystems, reducing ecosystem services for these environmental refugees, increasing their vulnerability, pushing them into abject poverty and decreasing levels of human well-being.

7.2 THE ROLE OF RAINWATER HARVESTING

Rainwater harvesting is one effective water technology for adaptation to increased variability in water supply and rainfall. Its decentralized nature allows the owners to benefit from direct management of demand as well as supply. With support technologies (modern and indigenous), rainwater harvesting is cost effective, and can release capital needed in times of disasters of surprising magnitudes. There also are savings of costs related to rainwater harvesting using simple processes and therefore infrastructure, including the pumps and energy inputs needed. This also reduces greenhouse gas emissions related to water supplies. Rainwater harvesting technology can therefore contribute to both climate change mitigation and adaptation.

Rainwater harvesting reducing CO_2 emissions?

The Fourth Assessment Report of the IPCC itself indicated that the expanded use of rainwater harvesting and other "bottom-up" technologies have the potential of reducing emissions by around 6 Gt CO_2 equivalent/year in 2030 (IPCC, 2007).

The system of water delivery in the context of current infrastructure development is part of the contributing system for green house gas emissions. The study of Flower et al. (2007) suggested that the main public water systems contribute to climate change by direct emissions of green house gases from water storage reservoirs and water treatment processes and through significant energy and material uses in the system. A case study from Melbourne, Australia, showed that appliances associated with residential end users of water have higher green house gas emissions than all upstream-downstream emissions. The contribution of an urban water system to climate change comes from three sources: consumption of energy derived from carbon-based fuels, bio-diesel processes which directly generated green house gases and consumption of goods and services that involve energy consumption or biochemical generation of green house gases. The total mass of green house gas emission associated with the end user of water including upstream and downstream activities was calculated as 7,146 kg CO_2-equivalents per household per year. If we compare this carbon footprint with the most common reference made on the gas emissions of fuel used in driving a car, the car's green house gas emissions are only 4,500 kg CO_2-equivalents each year per 15,000 miles, according to the Australian Greenhouse Office. In a study of the rainwater harvesting carbon footprint in New Zealand, the green house gas emissions from the use of a rainwater tank system was estimated at 2,300 kg CO_2 equivalents per household per year (Mithraratne and Vale, 2007). Different combinations of tanks with demand management affects the size of the CO_2 equivalent emissions related to the rainwater harvesting system used.

In Melbourne, another study was undertaken to come up with a method for achieving a climate-neutral Water Saving Framework (Blunt and Holt, 2007). It was found that potable water, using rainwater and other conservation devices, generates 0.173 CO_2t/ml while a wastewater treatment plant or wastewater recycling plant generates 0.875 CO_2t/ml. Thus, saving water can save green house gas emissions. In addition, substantial green house gas savings could be made by addressing wastewater management, in addition to the rainwater harvesting intervention.

In a case of a German industrial company (Appendix II: Case 7.4) rainwater harvesting lowered CO_2 emissions and energy and water costs. Huttinger Elektronik equipped its two-storey production and office building, built on 34,000 m² lot, with the following improvements:

- cooling towers for cooling work spaces

- rainwater for washing the company's street cars,

- rainwater for flushing toilets

- rain gardens through which excess rainwater percolated into the ground

- rainwater for the spray system of the re-cooling units of the building

- well water for cooling the offices

- rainwater for irrigation and evaporation purposes.

- cool water distributed through a double-pipe system without the customary refrigeration machinery.

With the above combination of technologies, based on the use of rainwater, the company was able to save the equivalent cost of energy corresponding to 56,664 litres a year of heating oil or a reduction of an equivalent of 318 tonnes of CO_2. In the case of using rainwater for cooling purposes, the savings amounted to 98,147 litres of heating oil with an equivalent reduction in CO_2 emissions of 551 tonnes (König, 2008). This computation of CO_2 emission equivalents is limited to the savings generated by fuel oil used and has not included the impacts on other parts of the production system.

Current adaptation strategies to climate variability and ecosystem management

Finding No. 3 of the Millennium Ecosystem Assessment stated that the degradation of ecosystem services could grow significantly worse during the first half of this century and that such degradation is a barrier to achieving the Millennium Development Goals. However, Finding No. 4 stated that, *"The challenge of reversing the degradation of ecosystems while meeting increasing demands for their services can be partially met under some scenarios that the MA considered, but these involve significant changes in policies, institutions, and practices that are not currently under way. Many options exist to conserve or enhance specific ecosystem services in ways that reduce negative trade-offs or that provide positive synergies with other ecosystem services"* (MA, 2005). It is also expected that many ecosystem services will be more vulnerable and fragile as climate change affects rainfall patterns and increases surface temperatures. Rainwater harvesting will continue to be one way to adapt to these increased changes in water supply and rainfall variability in the future, and, at the same time, enhance ecosystem services.

Several illustrations and case studies have been presented in the previous chapters, which highlight the contributions of rainwater harvesting to adaptation to the local challenges of water, healthy ecosystem services and human well-being. These and other cases will continue to serve as examples of adaptation strategies to climate variability, with multiple benefits. In the Philippines (Appendix II: Case 7.1), farmers in rainfed areas who use rainwater collected in ponds were able to raise their production yields from an average of 2.2 tons/hectare to an average of 3.3 tons/hectare with a high of 4.68 tons/hectare. The average yield from irrigated lands in the area is 3.3 tons/hectare. Considering the development costs of dams and irrigation canals, the government spends about US$5,000 to irrigate one hectare of land. A farmer may spend around US$400 to water one hectare of rice land. Added to the cost of the infrastructure could be the value of lost farm land, made into an irrigation pond, which the farmers estimated to be a loss equal to about 300 kilograms of rice (Salas, 2008).

Many experiences documented how rainwater harvesting conserved groundwater. The Ghogha project in rural Gujarat, India (Appendix II: Case 7.2) reported having successfully recharged the groundwater using 276 recharge structures in 82 villages (Khurana and Seghal,). India maintains a Central Groundwater Board which oversees artificial recharge of groundwater both in rural and urban areas. According to Singh (2001), the green revolution in Punjab and Haryana contributed significantly to India's food security but at the expense of soil and water degradation. The increase in groundwater use for agriculture between 1965 and 1995 resulted in a groundwater table decline of 2 meters. Alarmed by this situation, the Central Ground Water Authority planned for groundwater recharge and rooftop rainwater harvesting in another rainwater harvesting project in India. The Central Ground Water Authority reported that an additional 215 billion m^3 of groundwater can be generated by harvesting and recharging only 11% of the surplus runoff.

Drinking water is another product of ecosystem services. As a result of the decline in the earth's freshwater ecosystems and the related socio-economic factors, 1.1 billion people do not have access to improved water supplies and more than 2.6 billion lack access to improved sanitation. Also, water demand has increased and water supply has decreased. The ratio of water use to accessible supply increases by 20% every ten years (MA, 2005). Rainwater harvesting can help communities adapt to the declining availability of drinking water as droughts affect more semi-arid areas and floods inundate water sources and centralized water systems. The Thai Royal Government declared a policy of water resources development in 1979 to improve people's well-being and adapt to current rainfall variability (Appendix II: Case 7.5). The program supported construction of jars and tanks for augmenting drinking water supplies. Because of this program, the country was the first to attain water sufficiency during that water decade. After 10 years, 8 million tanks had been constructed. Most households have 1 ferrocement tank, a Thai jar and a membership in a community tank group. Private sector competition brought prices down and increased market availability of jars. However, education lagged behind and incidences of diarrhea became prevalent as health measures for keeping the tanks potable were not followed (Ariyabandu, 2001). A lesson to be learned is that when business interests are strong, government control over standards and community vigilance must be monitored.

The 1981 rainwater catchment systems program in Capiz, Philippines (Appendix II: Case 7.3) was accepted by local governments and the communities. The data from 2002 taken by the Planning and Development Office of the province showed an average of 67.5% the population using rainwater in 10 towns with inadequate groundwater resources. Three towns registered the 90% mark for the population using rainwater, according to the Planning and Development Office. The adoption of rainwater harvesting was a necessity to enable high quality water for domestic supply, as the groundwater was too low and sometimes too saline, and local springs were often contaminated by pollutants including agrochemicals (Salas, 2003).

The cases have shown that rainwater harvesting can make significant contributions to Millennium Development Goal No. 7 to ensure environmental sustainability. For example, the contribution of a decentralized water system such as rainwater harvesting to green house gas emission is far less than that of the current centralized water systems being used. Rainwater harvesting can contribute to water pollution control by capturing rain and using it or recharging it to groundwater. With rainwater being used, more surface water is conserved for use in aquatic ecosystem services and less groundwater is extracted. Use of rainwater harvesting for agro-forestry, in the forests, and on farms reduces soil erosion which is beneficial to the soils as well as to downstream water users.

Flood-damaged main pipe for potable water for the City of Iloilo.   Kahublagan

After the flood at Tigum-Aganan Watershed Philippines.   Kahublagan

Can rainwater harvesting mitigate soil erosion, which is one of the big drivers of ecosystems degradation? Terraces (*in situ* rainwater harvesting technologies) in the Philippines have been key rainwater harvesting technologies used especially in the upland and rainfed agricultural areas. They have helped control erosion. The recent typhoon (June 2007) which ravaged Panay Island and the landslides that brought down uprooted trees from the old growth forest in the mountains into the cities on the coast, showed how terraced hillsides could have withstood the landslides and excessive rains. In the experience of the Tigum-Aganan Watershed, Philippines, the flood crisis turned into a water crisis as the city's main water supply pipe from the watershed broke down. The problem continued to linger as more silt was carried by the river even 6 months after the flooding. As a result, the business of trucking water from various deep wells flourished. The urban poor suffered the most from the disrupted water supply service. Households with rainwater tanks were less affected by the water crisis. The farmers suffered too as they could not use silted irrigation water for their farms. But there were farmers who had adopted rainwater harvesting techniques who had adequate water for drinking and for growing crops during the cropping season. Those who had not adopted rainwater harvesting facilities missed a growing season.

Water purification is another ecosystem service rendered by the regulating function of water flowing through the landscape. Generally, the water purification function of ecosystem services is declining, according to the Millennium Ecosystem Assessment (MA, 2005). One source of polluted water is stormwater runoff. A recent practice is to collect rainwater to prevent stormwater from bringing pollution down the drainage ways and the sewer or directly into the river and the seas. Urbanization leads to significant changes in hydrology and pollutant transport from catchments which could harm sensitive aquatic ecosystems. An example to address the stormwater pollution in urban design is to introduce stormwater harvesting above the wetlands in Wyong-Warnervale, Australia (Leinster and White, 2007). The design was effective in assisting the water purification process and stormwater management.

The increasing risk of natural and man-made catastrophic events has been a growing niche for water provision in a decentralised manner with limited costs. In northern Bihar, India, recurrent floods turned communities into temporary migrants, with insufficient supplies of potable water. They traditionally had abundant water supplies as a result of the multiple floods, so rainwater harvesting was not an indigenous coping strategy to access drinking water. However, when flooding occurs, wells are contaminated by floodwater. By implementing low-cost rainwater harvesting for drinking and sanitation purposes, communities and individuals stay healthy during times of crisis (Appendix II: Case 7.3). After a famine in Turkana (1980), in the northwest of Kenya, the people's priority was construction of rainwater tanks after the immediate need for food was satisfied. ITDG got involved in the design of a system that would utilize any type of surface for catching water. When project fund was exhausted, the community started building stone lines and grass strips to catch water. The level of innovation was high in this Turkana community, given the flexibility of rainwater

Simple rain water harvesting can supply clean drinking water in times of flooding in Bihar   Prasad

harvesting as a water supply technique. It was learned that rainwater harvesting tanks, more than modern water equipment, are necessary life support systems in new settlements for the refugees (Barton, 2009).

7.3 THE ROLE OF RAINWATER HARVESTING FOR CLIMATE CHANGE ADAPTATION IN DOMESTIC WATER SUPPLY

Prof. George Kuczera of the University of Newcastle (2007) studied the impact of roofwater harvesting used to supplement public water supplies in an urban setting in Sydney, Australia. He stressed the fact that water reservoirs were vulnerable to prolonged drought and climate change which reduces rainfall amounts in catchments. The consequences of such occurrences for a large urban area could be catastrophic. In Sydney, the annual rainfall average is 900 mm to 1,200 mm. The study aimed at providing insights on the drought security performance of an integrated regional water supply and roofwater harvesting system. The base scenario, with 800 GL/year annual demand, suggested that a prolonged 10-year drought could bring about a complete failure of the system. However, with 50% of the households having a 5,000 litre rainwater tank, the probability that there will be a restriction of demand would be 8.5% to 5.2% in any year. The probability of any household running out of water in any given year would be 0.05% to 0.02%. With a backup desalination plant, the integrated system survived the 10-year drought. The study arrived at the conclusion that roof-water harvesting can make a substantial contribution as an adaptation technology and reduce the vulnerability of water supply in urban areas.

Working from the results of earlier studies on centralized water supplies (Coombes and Kuzera, 2003; Coombes and Lucas, 2006), a follow-on study proceeded to look into the efficiency of two types of water catchments in the climate change scenarios of Brisbane, Sydney, Melbourne and Perth. The result, with the exception of Perth, was that catchments exhibited a disproportionate decrease in yield in response to rainfall reductions as compared to the yields from the rainwater tanks. The authors concluded that the analysis strongly suggested that there is a significant difference in the response to climate change of the two systems for collecting water from rooftops or from catchments. The centralized water catchment systems supplying dams were seen as more sensitive, particularly in reduced runoff during reduced runoff periods, and hence potentially more susceptible to failure.

A number of cases on rainwater harvesting illustrate rainwater harvesting as an effective strategy to reduce vulnerability amongst local users to an unexpected lack of water. This suggests that one adaptation strategy to both short- and long-term variability in rainfall should be to actively work on decentralized water storage technologies, flexible to adopt and adapt in multiple user contexts. Joining the praises for rainwater harvesting is the Executive Director of the United Nations Environment Programme who declared:

▶ "As we look into what Africa can do to adapt to climate change … rainwater harvesting is one of those steps that does not require billions of dollars, that does not require international conventions first – it is a technology, a management approach, to provide water resources at the community level."

Indeed, rainwater harvesting has come of age. The technology has matured and the world condition is in such state that it needs this technology to heal itself, to protect what natural assets that have remained, and to start anew, beginning with the simplicity and appropriateness of this humble technology.

7.4 RECOMMENDATIONS AND KEY MESSAGES

Various studies have shown the positive values and opportunities offered by rainwater harvesting which could be harnessed by people to help face periods of severe variability in weather and other geophysical events, such as those predicted under the various scenarios of climate change. Climate and culture are inextricably linked (Pandey et al., 2003). Changes in climate will eventually change people's ways of doing things, but hopefully not with much suffering and pain. Changes in ways of doing things could be introduced gently in the way people live, as in the case of using rainwater harvesting to supplement or provide water supplies. We need to actively develop adaptation measures, as well as continue with mitigation efforts, to meet the challenges of water supply and demand in a future of climate change. Rainwater harvesting already provides cost efficient adaptation to variable supplies of water.

While there are abundant examples of rainwater harvesting in developed and developing contexts, for multiple purposes, there is still a lack of synthesised information: what are the investment costs? Who gains and who loses? Which impacts on the biophysical and social economic systems were positive? To answer these and other questions, there is a need to "stock up" on knowledge products for dissemination to all levels of end users. The momentum gained to date must be relentlessly sustained by network building.

Enabling policies for rainwater harvesting uptake and implementation are a first step for increased adoption. To move from a centralized to a decentralized water system, for example, is not an impossible task but one that needs sustained efforts of rationalization, planning, implementation and adjustment. It is recommended that responsible global bodies take on the task of assisting countries to mainstream rainwater harvesting in their policy agendas. This effort should be supported by education, technical exchanges, and capacity building efforts which are institutionalized to assist countries who are ready to venture onward with a change in the historic paradigm and culture for water availability and climate change protection. However, such changes should be undertaken from a position of understanding and knowledge of the potential benefits and risks of using rainwater harvesting, including the human benefits and environmental costs of diverting flows from surface and ground waters.

REFERENCES

Ariyabandu, R.D.S. 2001. Rainwater Jar Programme in North East Thailand. DTU, UK

Barton, T. Rainwater Harvesting in Turkana: water case study. Practical Action Consulting website last accessed January 2009

Blunt, S., Holt, P. 2007. Climate Neutral Water Saving Schemes. Rainwater and Urban Design Conference, IRCSA XIII Conference. Sydney, Australia,

Flower, D.J.M., Mitchell, V.G., Codner, G.P. 2007. Urban water systems: Drivers of climate change?

Rainwater and Urban Design 2007, IRCSA XIII Conference. Sydney, Australia,

Global Environment Outlook: environment for development (GEO 4). 2007. A report of the United Nations, UNEP/Progress Press, Malta

IPCC. 2007. Summary for Policymakers: An Assessment of the Intergovernmental Panel for Climate Change, Valencia Spain

Kuczera, G. 2007. Reginal Impacts of Roofwater Harvesting – Supplementing Public Water Supply. Paper presented at the Rainwater Colloquium in Kuala Lumpur, Malaysia

Khurana, I., Sehgal, M. Drinking Water Source Sustainability and Ground water Quality Improvement in Rural Gujarat, Mainstreaming Rainwater Harvesting IRCSA conference. Loc. cit.

Leinster, S., White, G. 2007. Stormwater to the Rescue: Regional Stormwater Harvesting for Ecosystem Protection and Potable Water Yield." Rainwater and Urban Design Conference, IRCSA XIII Conference. Sydney, Australia, August, 2007

Millennium Ecosystems Assessment. 2005: Ecosystems and Human Well-being Synthesis. Island Press. Washington D.C.

Mithraratne, N., Vale, R. 2007. Rain Tanks or Reticulated Water Supply? Rainwater and Urban Design 2007, IRCSA XIII Conference. Sydney, Australia,

Pandey, D.N., Gupta, A.K., Anderson, D.M. 2003. Rainwater harvesting as an adaptation to climate change. Current Science. Vol. 85:1

Salas, J.C. 2003. An Exploratory Study on Rainwater Harvesting in the Philippines: A Report to the World Bank.

Salas, J.C. 2008. Report to the Tigum Aganan Watershed Management Board. Iloilo City Philippines.

Singh, R.B. 2001. Impact of Land Use Change on Ground Water in Punjab and Haryana Plains. Impact of Human Activity on Groundwater Dynamics, Hans Gehrels *et al.*, (Eds). IAHS, Oxfordshire, UK

CHAPTER 8

SUMMARY OF CHAPTERS AND CASE STUDIES

Author: Jennie Barron, Stockholm Environment Institute, York, UK/Stockholm Resilience Centre, Stockholm, Sweden

8.1 POSITIVE EFFECTS RAINWATER HARVESTING AND ECOSYSTEM SERVICES

Healthy ecosystems provide a range of essential human well-being products and services. The water supply is essential both for human well-being and for productive ecosystem services. In this publication, rainwater harvesting has been discussed from an ecosystem perspective. The emerging picture is that different rainwater harvesting interventions can have positive effects both on ecosystem services and human well-being, thereby creating synergies in desired and positive development paths.

The positive effects of rainwater harvesting are related to the increased provisioning capacity of the ecosystem services. The primary services are the provision of more water of better quality for domestic supply and for increased crop production (Fig. 8.1). Secondary benefits relate to the regulating and supporting ecosystem services (Fig. 8.2). The three key services mentioned are: (1) reduced soil erosion improved infiltration capacity into the soil, and reduced incidences of flash floods/downstream flooding (2) recharge of shallow groundwater, springs and stream flows, and (3) increased species diversity amongst flora and fauna. In addition, some cases have discussed the positive impacts of rainwater harvesting through noting the reduced energy requirements (in terms of reduced CO_2 emissions) of rainwater harvesting as compared to conventional water supply technologies. An important but not always mentioned affect is on the aesthetic and cultural ecosystem services, where rainwater harvesting has improved both rural and urban area vegetation for improved human well-being.

In a few case the trade-off effect is discussed (e.g., Athi River, Kenya; Gansu, China). In these cases, rainwater harvesting does impact local water flows, possibly reducing water flows downstream through the consumptive use of the harvested rainfall. However, the authors point out that, although no cost-benefit analyses have been done, the additional pressures likely to have been introduced by withdrawing water from surface and ground water sources would have had even greater negative impacts on ecosystem services. Thus, it is recognised that a trade-off may have to be negotiated. Rainwater harvesting is no 'silver bullet' but the cases and experiences reported here indicate that it can have several benefits that may off-set the potential negative impacts.

The chapters and cases suggest that the area of most promise of benefit from rainwater harvesting is that of domestic supply in rural developing areas, where livelihoods are closely linked to local landscape production. Rainwater harvesting for domestic supply appears in all cases to have positive impacts on a range of human well-being indicators as well as on ecosystem services. Especially provisioning capacity improves, both through access to harvested water, but also through the different *in situ* interventions that recharge the soil and shallow groundwater systems. The increased storage of water often enables women, in particular, to increase small-scale gardening activities, improving diets, possibly health and very often incomes. The impacts on erosion control and reduced flooding/flash floods are mentioned as being desirable and positive.

A second area of positive benefit of rainwater harvesting on ecosystem services and human well-being is in urban areas. Here, the effects on ecosystem services are mainly related to reduced pressures for withdrawals from groundwater and surface water, and reduced incidences of flooding downstream. The key human well-being effects are related to direct income gains (reduced costs for public or private water supply, and also reduced CO_2 emissions as rainwater harvesting reduces energy demands).

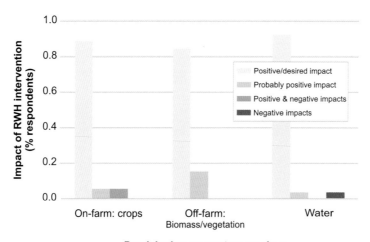

Figure 8.1: Summary of impacts on provisioning ecosystem services in the rainwater harvesting cases (n=27 cases, only respondent cases included, Appendix II)

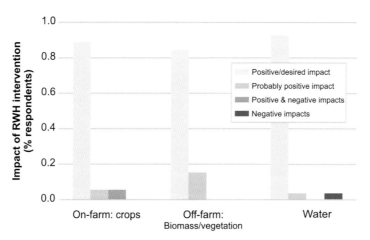

Figure 8.2: Summary of impacts on supporting/regulating ecosystem services in the rainwater harvesting cases (n=27 cases, only respondent cases included, Appendix II)

Even though most cases and chapters presented here reflect the positive gains in ecosystem services, there are also cases which report negative impacts through increased rainwater harvesting for consumptive uses, such as crop production or species cultivation that is more water intensive than previous crops. A caution for implementation of rainwater harvesting is warranted especially in increasingly water stressed locations. Here, additional rainwater harvesting may affect other uses of water, either for provisioning and supporting ecosystem services, and/or for withdrawals downstream. Implementation of rainwater harvesting for multiple purposes should be done with due assessments

of impacts both on the ecosystem services as well as human well-being.

8.2 HUMAN WELL-BEING IMPROVING WITH GAINS IN ECOSYSTEM SERVICES

Human well-being gains are evident as the ecosystem services improve in response to changes in ecosystem provisioning and supporting capacities. In all cases, positive effects were mentioned, at least to one of the four categories of poverty, income, health and gender. However, more negative impacts were mentioned especially relating to health, gender and equity of labour

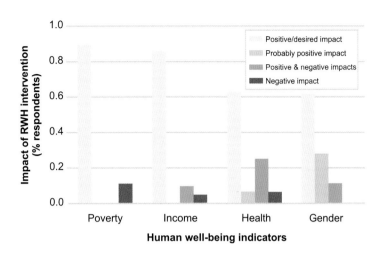

Figure 8.3: Summary of impacts on human well-being indicators in the rainwater harvesting cases (n=27 cases, only respondent cases included, Appendix II)

and increased income generated from the rainwater harvesting (Fig. 8.3). Although there may be negative effects on part of a community (determined by gender, income or land access, for example), no cases reported only negative effects on the four human well-being categories. An additional positive effect especially mentioned in the rainwater harvesting interventions for rural domestic and agricultural purposes at the farm-scale and watershed-scale was the building of human and social capital to undertake other development activities. When rainwater harvesting was implemented in a community, it also strengthened community coherence through the formation of interest groups, working groups or micro finance groups.

In addition, the decentralized nature of rainwater harvesting was mentioned as a positive side-effect, which reduced reliance on public (or private) water supply systems. This is advantageous both in rural areas, where scattered households make water supply service costly and sometimes nearly impossible (i.e., Gansu, China; North East Brazil) due to local biophysical conditions. It is also used as means of reducing vulnerability to interrupted water supply, especially in regions prone to earthquakes or other natural hazards that can disrupt public water supplies (Star City, South Korea; Sumida City, Japan; Capiz, Philippines).

Although the cost-benefit analyses are rarely available, the cases and chapters presented suggest that rainwater harvesting can be a comparatively inexpensive investment and fast option to improve not only human

well-being but also a range of ecosystem services, both directly and indirectly (Gansu, China; North East Thailand; Kaijado, Kenya; North East Brazil).

CHAPTER 9

KEY MESSAGES AND SUGGESTIONS

9.1 KEY MESSAGES

- Ecosystem services are fundamental for human well-being, and are the basis of rural livelihoods, particularly for the poor. Rainwater harvesting can serve as an opportunity to enhance ecosystem productivity, thereby improving livelihoods, human well-being and economies.

- Rainwater harvesting has been shown to create synergies between landscape management and human well-being. These synergies are particularly obvious when rainwater harvesting improves rainfed agriculture, is applied in watershed management, and when rainwater harvesting interventions address household water supplies in urban and rural areas.

- Rainwater harvesting has often been a neglected opportunity in water resource management: only water from surface and ground water sources are conventionally considered. Managing rainfall will also present new management opportunities, including rainwater harvesting.

- Improved water supply, enhanced agricultural production and sustainable ecosystem services can be attained through adoption of rainwater harvesting with relatively low investments over fairly short time spans (5-10 years).

- Rainwater harvesting is a coping strategy in variable rainfall areas. In the future climate change will increase rainfall variability and evaporation, and population growth will increase demand on ecosystem services, in particular for water. Rainwater harvesting will become a key intervention in adaptation and reducing vulnerabilities.

- Awareness and knowledge of ecosystem services must be increased amongst practitioners and policy makers alike, to realise the potentials of rainwater harvesting and ecosystem benefits for human well-being.

9.2 SUGGESTIONS

- Consider rainfall as an important, manageable resource in water management policies, strategies and plans. Then rainwater harvesting interventions can be included as potential options in land and water resource management activities for human well-being and ecosystem productivity.

- Realise that rainwater harvesting is not a 'silver bullet', but can be effective as a complementary and viable alternative to large-scale water withdrawals, and as a way of reducing the negative impacts on ecosystem services, not least in emerging water-stressed basins.

- Rainwater harvesting is a local intervention, with primarily local benefits on ecosystems and human livelihoods. Stakeholder consultations and public participation are key to enabling the negotiation of the positive and negative trade-offs that may emerge. Rainwater harvesting interventions should always be compared with alternative water management interventions and infrastructure investments.

- Access and the right to land can be a first step toward implementing rainwater harvesting. Special measures should be in place so rainwater harvesting benefits the land-poor and the landless in communities.

- Establish enabling policies and cost–sharing strategies (including subsides) to be provided together with technical know-how and capacity building.

ACKNOWLEDGEMENTS

This report was funded jointly by UNEP and SEI. Grants were provided by FORMAS. In addition, DHI, supported key activities in the preparation. We would like to thank the chapter authors, and the contributing authors for their input to this publication. The editor and authors are especially grateful for the reviewer comments

APPENDIX I

RAINWATER HARVESTING CASE INFORMATION: INDICATORS ON ECOSYSTEM SERVICES AND HUMAN WELL-BEING

	Provisioning On-farm: cn	Off-farm:	water	Supporting /regulating -soil	-water	-biodiversity	Aesthetic & GHG emmi	HUMAN WELLBEING INDICATORS Poverty	Income	Health	Gender
1 India, Madyah Pradesh	+	+	+	+	+			+	+	+?	+?
2 Denmark, Arhus		+	+		+	+?	+		-?	-?	
3 India, Karnataka			-		.						
4 South Africa??											
5 India, Sukhomairi	+/-	+	+?	+	+	+	+	+/-	+/-	+	+
6 Kenya, Athi flower	+	+	+?	+	+/-	+/-	+/-	+	+		+
7 Tanzania, Makanya	+	+	+	+	+	+	+/-	+	+	+/-	+/-
8 Morocco, Sekkouma-Irzaine	+	+	+	+	+	+	+				+?
9 Mauretania, Assaba-Kiffa	+	+	+	+	+	+	+	+	+		+
10 Southern Africa Miombo		+	+	+	+	+					
11 West Africa: parklands	+	+	+	+	+	+	+?	+	+		+?
12 Burkina Faso	+	+	+	+	+						
13 Kenya, Kaiiado	+	+?	+	+	+			+	+	+	+
14 Kenya	+		+			+		+	+	+	+
15 Uganda	+		+		+				+		+
16 Brazil, NE semi-arids	+	+	+	+	+	+	+	+	+	+	+
17 China, Gansu	+	+	+	+	+	+	+	+	+	+	+?
18 South Korea, Star city			+		+	+			+	+	
19 Germany, Bavaria			+		+	+	+?		+	+	
20 Germany, Knittlingen			+	+	+	+	+?		+	+/-	
21 Japan, Sumida City	+		+	+	+	+	+?				
22 Taiwan, Taipei	+		+	+	+	+			+		
23 Australia Svdnev			+		+		+			+	
24 Philippines, Tigum Aganan	+	+	+	+/-	+	+/-	+		+/-	+	+/-
25 Philippines, Capiz	+		+	+	+	+?	+		+	+	+
26 India, Bihar			+	+	+	+				+	
27 Germany, Freiburg			+	+	+	+					
28 Thailand	+?	+?	+	+	+	+			+	+/-	+?